"Calling a **ravenous bird** from the east, the man that executeth my counsel from a **far country**: yea, I have spoken it, I will also bring it to pass; I have purposed it, I will also do it".

-Isaiah 46:11

# The Apostolic is a means to the end...

The Church is the Body, Bride, and embodiment of God's purpose for humanity, fully engaged in His Kingdom mission.

**The Apostolic** is the empowering means or energy in how we accomplish His Kingdom purpose.

**The Kingdom** is our purposed destiny from our creation: The rule, reign, and presence of God.

"Apostolic is not a MOVEMENT, it is only a MEANS!"

Beloved, we are the light of the world. By our very spiritual nature, we are called to lead from the front!

Dan Evangelist Jones III is an anointed servant, called by God at an early age to minister to His people. For over 30 years, he has been graced to serve in various leadership and support roles within the Body of Christ. He has served as a deacon, counselor, assistant pastor, elder, department director, and has shepherded a congregation. Additionally, he brings more than 50 years of combined leadership experience in the military, church, and corporate sectors to the Body of Christ.

The Holy Spirit has anointed him to stand in various ministry offices and has endowed him with the gift of teaching. From early on, he promised God, "If You would teach me, I will teach Your people." I submit to you today that my anointing and zeal are to teach and serve the Body of Christ. I have a deep passion to see the Church flow apostolically into her Kingdom mandate. I am inspired to teach foundational truths that break the bondage of traditionalism—truths that keep many from walking in the fullness of God's will for their lives.

Dan Jones is the assistant pastor at Breakthrough Harvest Church and the founder of Revealed Ministry, an apostolic leadership ministry that provides a wide array of services to the Kingdom. These include leadership and prophetic summits, basic leadership and management training, Kingdom principles training, and foundational biblical education.

He is a member of ACTS: The Apostolic Council of Transformational Servant Leaders, led by Dr. Ron Cottle. He holds a Master of Theology degree from the Christian Life School of Theology in Columbus, Georgia.

Dan Jones stands ready to serve the Body through his God-given gifts. His desire to see other leaders' visions fulfilled outweighs his personal ambitions. His heart's deepest desire is to teach God's people about God.

**Author:** [Dan Evangelist Jones III]

Copyright © [Original Year], [2010]
Revised Edition © [2025], [Dan Evangelist Jones III]

All rights reserved. No part of this publication may be reproduced, distributed, or transmitted in any form or by any means, including photocopying, recording, or other electronic or mechanical methods, without the prior written permission of the publisher, except in the case of brief quotations embodied in critical reviews and certain other noncommercial uses permitted by copyright law.

ISBN: 979-8-89940-228-9

**Cover Design:** Fiverr: **Rehan Graphics**

This is a revised and expanded edition of a work originally published in 2010.

**Note on This Edition**

This edition of *The Foundational Apostolic Workbook* has been revised and updated to reflect new insights, refined language, and expanded sections. Originally published in [2010], this version includes grammar improvements, strengthen sentence statements, adding information to paragraphs improving statements, clarity.

The following books were references for some subject quotes:
Apostles and the Emerging Apostolic Movement
David Cannistraci

The Last Apostles on Earth
Roger Sapp

The following Bible translations were used in compiling this book:
    King James Version, New International Version
    New Living Translation, Amplified Version
    New King James Version
Blueletterbible.com translations and Strong's concordance were used in compiling this book.

**Dan Evangelist Jones** does not subscribe to any apostolic denomination or ministry. This ministry stands on, preaches, and teaches foundational biblical principles. **DEJ** derives his vision solely from the Bible as God's authority and from the ascension gift of the apostle.

**DEJ** does not take away from any ministry, church, or organization that identifies as apostolic. On the contrary, our mission is to teach, train, and further equip those who are seeking a deeper understanding of their purpose in God.

My apostolic vision for the Body of Christ is to **equip, empower, and elevate** those whom God allows us to connect with. Our prayer is that you and your calling into the apostolic will bear the fruit that God has ordained for you.

May every barrier that could hinder you be removed and may the power of His resurrection be revealed in you and through the people connected to your call. In Jesus name. Amen

# Table of Contents

| | |
|---|---|
| FAT-000 | Cover Sheet |
| FAT-001 | The Roadblocks to a Flourishing Apostolic Ministry |
| FAT-100 | Apostolic Identity: Understanding Apostles and the Apostolic Mandate |
| FAT-200 | The Great Commission |
| FAT-300 | The Apostolic Government |
| FAT-400 | Faith Imperative |
| FAT-500 | False Apostle |
| FAT-600 | Kingdom Unity: The Fruit of Apostolic Alignment |
| FAT-700 | Fellowship: The Missing Link |
| FAT-800 | Apostolic Company    (small group developing into AP company) |
| FAT-900 | Building Apostolic and Prophetic Teams |
| FAT-1000 | How to Properly Transition to an Apostolic Body (Leaders Only) |
| FAT-1100 | Apostolic Strategy (Seeing the battlefield) (Leaders Only) |
| FAT-1200 | Apostolic Church Structural Paradigm |
| FAT-1300 | The Heart of the Apostolic Message |
| FAT-1400 | Producing Apostolic Fruit (Leaders Only) |
| FAT-1500 | Apostolic kingdom |
| FAT-1600 | Why we Fail (not the church) |
| FAT-1700 | Requirements to become Apostolic |
| FAT-1800 | Your Specific Apostolic Sphere of Influence |

# The potential of the Church is limitless when she is truly guided by the Holy Spirit.

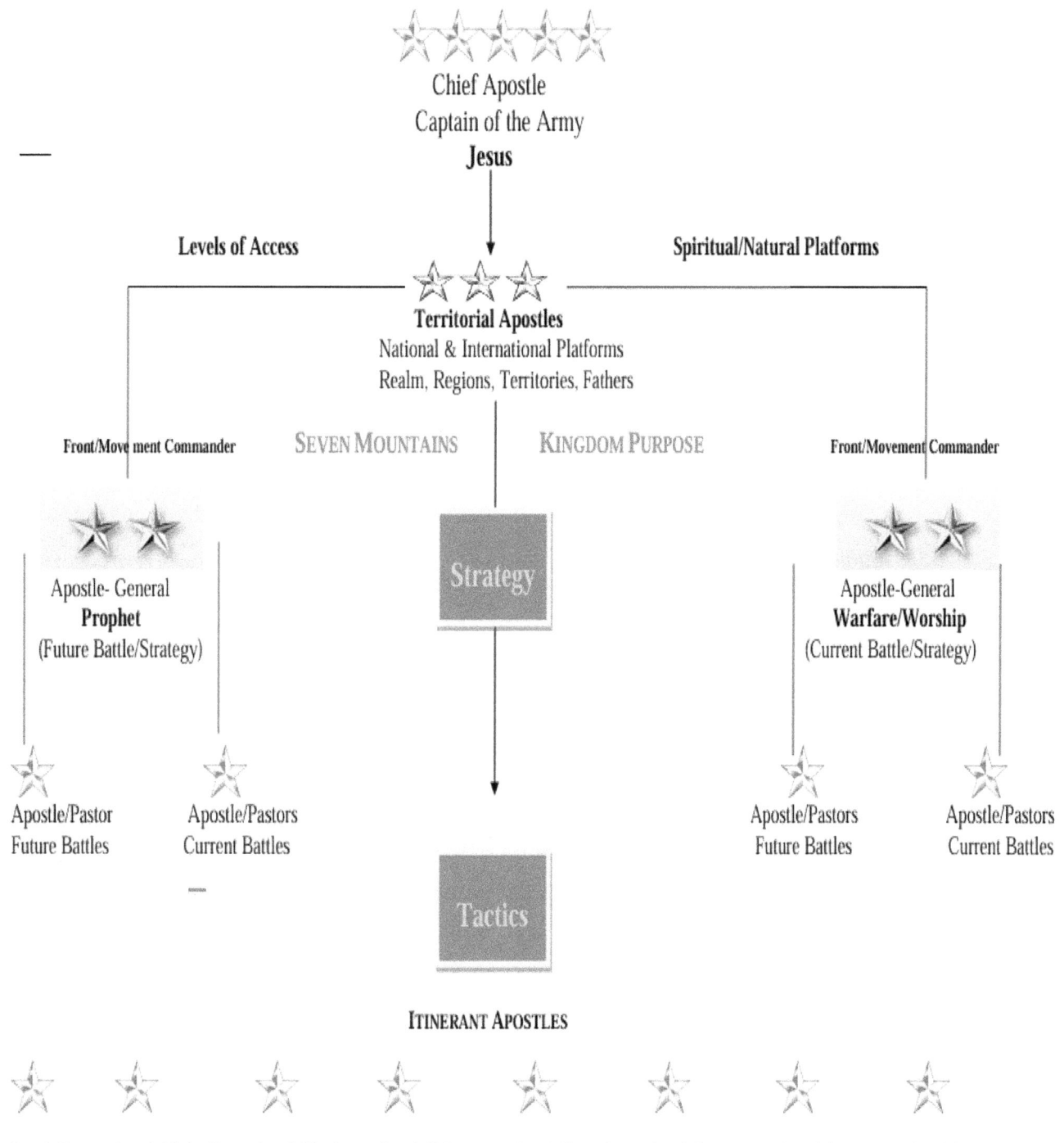

# Dan *Evangelist* Jones Ministry is sent to:

Who

- DEJM is called to teach apostolic and kingdom principles to churches and ministries that are bound by traditional mandates.
- DEJM is called to serve those in need of apostolic teaching and guidance.

What

- DEJM functions as part of the apostolic government outlined in *1 Corinthians 12:28*.
- DEJM is an apostolic teaching ministry.
- DEJM assists individuals and ministries transitioning from a traditional church model to an apostolic framework.
- DEJM primarily teaches apostolic doctrine, Kingdom principles, godly living, and foundational biblical truths.

Where

- DEJM is called to serve locally, nationally, and internationally as led by the Holy Spirit.
- DEJM ministers in churches, conferences, seminars, and various ministry gatherings, delivering the apostolic word to the Body of Christ.
- DEJM carries an apostolic mandate for both local and global platforms.
- DEJM also teaches in colleges, schools, or academic settings as opportunities arise.

When

- DEJM was born and released into active ministry in 2010. *(The vision continues to evolve as God leads.)*
- DEJM is presently active in equipping the Body of Christ in preparation for the return of our Lord.

F.A.T.-000

What Is the Apostolic—and How Should It Affect My Spiritual Life Today?

Today, when we look at the Church, we often see the Body of Christ bogged down by denominationalism, personal visions, religious empires, buildings, personalities, territorial mindsets, geographic limitations, and inner divisions, just to name a few. Because of these distractions, the Church is far from what it was intended to be and is unable to fulfill its true purpose in its current condition.

The apostolic is the understanding that *you*, as part of the Body of Christ, are sent called to a higher purpose than what is commonly seen today. It is a divine call from "here to there." Without the apostolic anointing, there is a lack of power and authority in the Body. If we're reading scripture correctly, we can see that something crucial is missing. With apostolic impartation, we begin to see from God's perspective and recognize that the doctrine of the apostles and of Christ Himself is vital for the Church to fulfill its mission.

The apostolic brings restoration and unity, two essential elements that are missing from much of today's ministry. This shift breaks the "me, mine, and I" mentality that dominates many churches and realigns them with God's purpose. When the apostolic is activated in your life, you recognize the role of the apostle and begin to clearly see the Great Commission as the great vision of the Church.

The apostolic empowers the Body with a Kingdom mandate. It creates an environment where biblical wonders, transformative deeds, salvation, unity, and restoration can take place. It gives the world an authentic witness of Christ.

The apostolic is more than a movement it is the initiative and energy of God revealed throughout Scripture. It is the original and primary purpose given to the Church. It is the full force of the Gospel released into the earth. It's the kind of power the world is searching for in the Church: God being God through His people, without restriction. When the leaders and members of the

Body of Christ truly realize that God's collective will cannot be accomplished without the apostolic, we will witness a supernatural release that will cause the lost to be saved and the Believer thriving in their walk in Christ.

Finally, and most importantly the apostolic is Jesus: His mission, His purpose, His obedience, and His works for the Church. The apostolic is His method for fulfilling the Great Commission. Tragically, in many places today, the Church is no longer centered on Jesus and the apostolic mission. And that absence is deeply felt.

What Is the Apostle or Apostolic? What Does It Have to Do with the Church and Her Purpose? What Does It Have to Do with Me?

## Apostolic:

The term "apostle" (noun) or "apostolic" (adjective) represents a God-ordained, New Testament paradigm in His redemptive plan. The apostle, the messenger, and the message are foundational (proton—first in order, precedence, and purpose). The apostolic call precedes the full realization of both the Church and the Kingdom.

The apostolic is the energy, authority, and divine action by which God's will is carried out, advancing His Kingdom and fulfilling His Church's mission.

## Church:

The Church is a parenthetical purpose in God's redemptive plan, inserted among His dealings with Israel and integrated into His overall Kingdom agenda.

While this topic is vast and well-documented in ecclesiastical writings, it's important to grasp that the Church is God's New Testament instrument. It serves as the carrier of His Kingdom purpose.

The Church is the Body of Christ, destined to become the Bride of Christ. In the present age, she functions as a servant in the Kingdom of God, performing priestly and administrative roles as part of her divine assignment.

Kingdom:

The Kingdom of God is one of the most under-taught and under-understood subjects in the modern Church. As a result, we have raised generations of believers unaware of their identity, destiny, and divine purpose.

If you do not understand the Kingdom, you will not fully grasp the purpose of the Church. And without a foundation in those two truths, the apostolic won't make complete sense either. To help bridge this gap, I've developed a workbook titled "Apostolic-Kingdom" to align and connect the Church's mission with its apostolic and Kingdom mandate.

Think on this:
1 Corinthians 15:24 says, *"Then cometh the end, when He shall have delivered up the Kingdom to God..."*
This verse shows the Son is sent apostolically, coming to redeem His Father's Kingdom and return it to Him. The Gentile Church plays a vital part in that redemptive process.

*"Influence is the power of the Apostle and Apostolic"*

Course Name:  The Roadblocks to a Flourishing Apostolic Ministry
Course Number:  FAT-001
Course Objective:  To address the various issues that hinder the office of the apostle and the apostolic movement.

1. Traditionalism

    Traditionalism will be one of the 'thorn in the side' issues discussed throughout this workbook.

A.  Traditionalism is defined as:

   A1.  Wikipedia
        Traditional values, those beliefs, moral codes, and morals that are passed down from generation to generation.

   A2.  Dictionary.com
        Adherence to tradition as authority, especially in matters of religion.

B.  Scriptural Examples:

   Mark 7:8 KJV
   For laying aside the commandment of God, ye hold the tradition of men, as the washing of pots and cups: and many other such like things ye do.

   Mark 7:9 KJV
   And he said unto them, Full well ye reject the commandment of God, that ye may keep your own tradition.

   Mark 7:13 KJV
   Making the word of God of none effect through your tradition, which ye have delivered: and many such like things do ye.

Colossians 2:8 KJV

Beware lest any man spoil you through philosophy and vain deceit, after the tradition of men, after the rudiments of the world, and not after Christ.

1 Peter 1:18 KJV

Forasmuch as ye know that ye were not redeemed with corruptible things, as silver and gold, from your vain conversation received by tradition from your fathers.

2. Hierarchy Leadership

Hierarchical leadership is one of the formidable strongholds within the Church that prevents the apostolic move of God.

First, we must acknowledge that there is a positive hierarchy and order to all things of God, including the Church. However, in this Apostolic Workbook, we are addressing the negative impact of territorial hierarchical leadership that is set in its ways, preventing the flow of the Holy Spirit and hindering the apostolic paradigms within the Body.

Hierarchy is defined as:

Wikipedia
hierarchy (Greek: hierarchia (ἱεραρχία), from hierarches, "leader of sacred rites") is an arrangement of items (objects, names, values, categories, etc.) in which the items are represented as being "above," "below," or "at the same level as" one another

Dictionary.com
Hierarchy
1. Any system of persons or things ranked one above another.
2. Government by ecclesiastical rulers.
3. The power or dominion of a hierarch.

Luke 7:39 KJV

Now when the Pharisee which had bidden him saw it, he spake within himself, saying, this man, if he were a prophet, would have known who and what manner of woman this is that toucheth him: for she is a sinner.

- ➤ The mindset of a hierarchical structure is always presumptuous.

C. Examples and Attitudes of Hierarchical Leaders

Luke 11:38 KJV

And when the Pharisee saw it, he marvelled that he had not first washed before dinner.

- ➤ A hierarchical mindset operates with a spirit of religious order.

- ➤ This mindset prevents one from truly seeing and attaining their salvation, or from operating in a false sense of accomplishment.

Luke 18:11 KJV

The Pharisee stood and prayed thus with himself, God, I thank thee, that I am not as other men are, extortioners, unjust, adulterers, or even as this publican.

- ➤ Generally, a person with this type of mindset sees themselves better and above others.

Philippians 3:5 KJV

Circumcised the eighth day of the stock of Israel, of the tribe of Benjamin, an Hebrew of the Hebrews; as touching the law, a Pharisee.

➢ Here Paul uses an example of himself, as if he were boasting about his religious accomplishments.

➢ Hierarchy includes the systems or religious systems and mindsets of that person (s).

Matthew 23: 10-15

10 Neither be ye called masters: for one is your Master, even Christ. 11 But he that is greatest among you shall be your servant. 12 And whosoever shall exalt himself shall be abased; and he that shall humble himself shall be exalted. 13 But woe unto you, scribes and Pharisees, hypocrites! for ye shut up the kingdom of heaven against men: for ye neither go in yourselves, neither suffer ye them that are entering to go in. 14 Woe unto you, scribes and Pharisees, hypocrites! for ye devour widows' houses, and for a pretence make long prayer: therefore, ye shall receive the greater damnation. 15 Woe unto you, scribes and Pharisees, hypocrites! for ye compass sea and land to make one proselyte, and when he is made, ye make him twofold more the child of hell than yourselves.

➢ Master, under the spirit of hierarchy, embraces the "spirit to lord over others".

➢ This type of person or system prevents others from entering the Kingdom.

➢ Hierarchy leaders like the Pharisee actually shut Heaven.

➢ "The wrong type of hierarchical system destroys lives; it does not produce life.

3. Territorial Members

   Yourdictionary.com

   Territorial is defined as: of territory or land, characterized by or displaying territoriality.

The main objection to an apostolic or Kingdom 'shift' comes from territorial leaders and individuals. These people can be a significant hindrance to the advancement of the apostolic purpose of the Church.

3. Territorial Issues

   3.1 The Body's of Christ most common territorial objectors:

   | Leaders Issues | People Issues |
   |:---:|:---:|
   | Positions | Seating |
   | "My" Vision | Positional Authority |
   | Tenure | Tenure |
   | Legacy Pass-down | Relationships with leaders. |
   | Investing their knowledge in others | Rule Changes |
   | Changes | Structural Changes |

4. A Lack of Teaching

A lack of teaching is one of the greatest threats to the Body of Christ. Many believers are simply alone for the ride, unaware and uninterested in where they are going or why. This kind of mindset serves as fertile ground for territorial leaders and controlling systems to thrive.

Ecclesiastes 9:8
Let thy garments be always white; and let thy head lack no ointment.

Hosea 4:
6 My people are destroyed for lack of knowledge: because thou hast rejected knowledge, I will also reject thee, that thou shalt be no priest to me: seeing thou hast forgotten the law of thy God, I will also forget thy children.

Problems when there is no teaching:

a. Lack of directions.

b. Lack of directives.

c. Lack of wisdom

d. Lack of foresight and oversight.

e. Lack of purpose and destiny elevation.

5. Insecurity (leaders who are insecure as to who and what they are)

An insecure leader can be one of the greatest hindrances to an apostolic or Holy Spirit move.

5a. Examples of Insecurity People and Situations:

a. Moses needing Aaron    Exodus 4:10-16
b. Gideon                 Judges 6: 27,36-37, 39
c. King Saul with David   1 Samuel 18: 6-12, 19:1-2

Questions:

1. What was Moses' insecurity, and how does it hinder an apostolic move?

   _____
   _____
   _____

2. What was Gideon's insecurity, and how does it hinder an apostolic move?

   _____
   _____
   _____

3. What was King Saul's insecurity, and how does it hinder an apostolic move?

_____

_____

_____

Insecurity Strongholds

    a. Jealousness

    b. Self-esteem Issues

    c. Faithlessness

    d. Lack of Trust

    e. Introvert

6. Bad Experiences

Note: For the laity, bad experiences are one of the main issues that hinder them from moving forward into uncharted territory. These "bad experiences" often involve unpleasant people or situations that have left a lasting negative impact.

Bad Experiences Issues:

a. False Prophets (ministers) and leaders.

b. Lies (being lied to)

c. Abuse of Power

d. The improper employment of spiritual gifts.

e. Being singled out.

f. Dictator and territorial leaders.

g. Lording leaders (making people subjective)

h. Suppressive leaders.

| | |
|---|---|
| Course Name: | Apostolic Identity: Understanding Apostles and the Apostolic Mandate |
| Course Number: | FAT-100 |
| Course Objective: | To define the differences and characteristics of the office of an apostle and the apostolic call upon the Body. |

1. Definition of Apostle

   a. Apostle=   ap-os-tol-o

   Definition:  A delegate, specially, an ambassador of the Gospel; <u>officially a commissioner of Christ.</u> (apostle) (with miraculous powers) apostle, messenger, he that is sent.

   Strong's Concordance
   Apo= from    stello= to send:    Combine definition: "sent from"

   a. The apostle is one of the five-fold ministry gifts given for the leadership and development of the Church (Ephesians 4:12).

   b. The office of the apostle is specifically appointed by Jesus, given to individuals, set apart by the Holy Spirit, and affirmed by human leadership (Acts 13:1–4).

   c. The apostolic refers to the specific activation by the Holy Spirit for a person, church, ministry, business, or work aligned with God's purpose for the Church.

**2.** Apostolic is defined as:

    a. The Body of Christ is corporately sent (John 17:18; 20:21; Matthew 28:19).

    b. The apostolic is not an office, gift, or ministry position.

    c. It is the imparted energy of the Holy Spirit, coupled with the dispensation of grace for the Church, enabling her to fulfill her divine purpose.

**3.** The Theology of Sent.

    a. The concept of being "sent from" is key to properly understanding both the apostle's and the apostolic mission.

    b. The apostle's greatest duty or primary focus is the Great Commission, the very purpose for which they are sent (Matthew 28:19). The absence of this focus is a major missing element in much of today's church and leadership.

    c. Many leaders are known for their "sent" title, such as, "I'm a pastor," or "I'm a minister", but not for the purpose behind it. The title often precedes them, while purpose is rarely evident.

    d. The "from" in ministry always represents God. It speaks of Him, reveals His glory, tells His story, and always points back to Him and His ultimate purpose.

**4.** Old Testament types of Apostles (sent people)

    4.a    Adam: First Parents, Sent Parents

        Genesis 1:28

        And God blessed them, and God said unto them, Be fruitful, and multiply, and replenish the earth, and subdue it: and have dominion over the fish of the sea, and over the fowl of the air, and over every living thing that moveth upon the earth.

Subdue is a military term that reflects the "strategy" nature of the definition and mission of the term apostolic.

4.b    Abraham    First Apostolic- <u>Father</u> of Faith

> Genesis 12: 1-3
> Now the LORD had said unto Abram, Get thee out of thy country, and from thy kindred, and from thy father's house, unto a land that I will shew thee: 2 And I will make of thee a great nation, and I will bless thee, and make thy name great ; and thou shalt be a blessing: 3 And I will bless them that bless thee, and curse him that curseth thee: and in thee shall all families of the earth be blessed .

- Get thee out = The beginning of the apostolic-type call of Abraham and the chosen people of God.

- The call, ministry or summons of God is always apostolic in nature; it requires one to "go".

4.c    Moses  First Apostolic- <u>Deliverer</u>

> Exodus 3:12
> And he said, Certainly I will be with thee; and this shall be a token unto thee, that I have sent thee: When thou hast brought forth the people out of Egypt, ye shall serve God upon this mountain.

- Moses apostolic deliverance qualifies him by signs (token) and the fact that he was sent.

- The 'sent' aspect of Moses' ministry is consistently affirmed in Scripture, showing that he was sent by God as both an apostle and an apostolic deliverer.

4.d     The Quintessential Apostle: Jesus

1. Light and Life emanates from Him to Man

John 1:4
In Him was life, and the life was the light of men.

- Light emanates from Him into the world; His light has apostolic properties. 2 Co 4:6, John 1:4-5,7,9

- The light (Zoe) has apostolic purpose. Pro 6:23, Matt 5:14, Luke 1:79, Acts 13:47

2. His very purpose is "sent"

Luke 4:18
The Spirit of the Lord is upon me, because he hath anointed me to preach the gospel to the poor; he hath sent me to heal the brokenhearted, to preach deliverance to the captives, and recovering of sight to the blind, to set at liberty them that are bruised,

- Jesus was sent by the Father. Isa 61:1-2

- His apostolic instruction: heal the broken hearted: preach deliverance to the captives: recovering sight to the blind: and set at liberty them that are bruise. Isa 61:1-2

4.e    Jesus the <u>APOSTOLIC</u> personified

> Hebrew 3:1
> Wherefore, holy brethren, partakers of the heavenly calling, consider the Apostle and High Priest of our profession, Christ Jesus.
>
> ➢ There is only one apostle.
>
> ➢ All other apostles are delegated apostles or serve in a proxy capacity
>
> ➢ All other apostles operate under the only authorized mantle, the authority of Jesus. Heb 3:1, 1 Pet 2:6, Eph 4:15, Col 1:18

4.f    Jesus' Disciples Sent

John 20:21
Then said Jesus to them again, Peace be unto you: as my Father hath sent me, even so send I you.

- As He was sent, so are we. The disciples were not sent out loosely; they were disciples in training for the apostolic.

- If He had never been sent, we would have no basis for being sent, nor could we define a purpose for going.

- Example: Without the apostolic, there would be no Church, no vision, no salvation, no baptism, and no hope, all would be in vain.

5.   The Sending Authenticates You're Sent.

Jeremiah 14: 14-15
Then the LORD said unto me, the prophets prophesy lies in my name: *I sent them not*, neither have I commanded them, neither spake unto them: they prophesy unto you a false vision and divination, and a thing of nought, and the deceit of their heart. 15 Therefore thus saith the LORD concerning the prophets that prophesy in my name, and I sent them not, yet they say, Sword and famine shall not be in this land; By sword and famine shall those prophets be consumed.

- Every minister's gift should and does come from God. It was first sent, then given. Acts 2:38, 11:17, 1Cor 7:7, Eph 4:8-11

- Every ministry gift and ministry should be authenticated by God's word and for its truth.

Jeremiah 28:9
The prophet which prophesieth of peace, when the word of the prophet shall come to pass, then shall the prophet be known, that the LORD hath truly sent him.

- The truth of your "sent purpose" shall confirm who you are.

John 5:36    Works (sent to) authenticate.
But I have greater witness than that of John: for the works which the Father hath given me to finish, the same works that I do, bear witness of me, that the Father hath sent me.

- Even Jesus' works witnessed who He was.
- Your work should be witnessed to who you are. (You should not have to tell someone you are an apostle), Like Jesus; your works should witness (authenticates) what you are.

6. Apostle's Signs

   2 Corinthians 12:12
   Truly the signs of an apostle were wrought among you in all patience, in signs, and wonders, and mighty deeds.

   **a.** Patience equates to Character.
   The first important sign of an apostle or apostolic is (internal).
   (1) It is important for the person to be seasoned, learned and developed.

   **b.** Signs, wonders, and mighty deeds.
   The second important sign of an apostle or the apostolic is external.
   (1) Too often, this is prioritized or sought after before character is developed.

7. The Apostle's Seal

   1 Corinthians 9:2
   If I be not an apostle unto others, yet doubtless I am to you: for the seal of mine apostleship are ye in the Lord.

   **a.** Changed lives and transformed people are the true authentication of an apostle.

   b. You might not be and are not an apostle to everyone.

   c. If you do not have a life-changing relationship with someone, you are not their apostle.

8. Apostle's Responsibilities

   1. Developing Leaders. 2 Tim 2:1-2
   2. Overseeing and strengthening churches. Acts 20:28, 1 Tim 3:1

3. Fathering (leaders) within your realm of influence.

4. Care (heart & discernment) for the church, its people, and its purpose.
   Acts 6:2

a. Paul's Developing of Timothy (his spiritual son)

2 Timothy 2:22
Flee also youthful lusts: but follow righteousness, faith, charity, peace, with them that call on the Lord out of a pure heart.

- Main job of the apostle is to train and develop sons of the faith. Gen 18:17,19, Mal 4:5-6, Luke 1:17, Phil 2:22

- Apostles should be teachers of God's children, His people, and potential leaders.

- The foundational anointing or mindset of an apostle's heart is their apostolic purpose.

b. Overseeing and Strengthening Churches

2 Corinthians 11:28
Beside those things that are without, that which cometh upon me daily, the care of all the churches.

Overseeing & Strengthening Responsibilities:

1. Developing, establishing, and expounding upon church doctrine. Eph 2:20, Isa 28:9, Acts 2:42, 1Tim 4:6

2. Installing leaders (Elders) in churches you establish and in your realms of influence.

3. Managing and conducting spiritual warfare for your apostolic realm of assignment.

   ➢ As an apostle or apostolic leader, your responsibility is primarily for the daily care of the church (church universal: not necessarily local), specifically in strategic areas.

   ➢ Anything beyond that means you're operating in a pastoral role or some form of pastoral leadership, with direct authority over others.

c. Establishing AP Doctrine

   (1) Acts 2:42
   And they continued stedfastly in the apostles' doctrine and fellowship, and in breaking of bread, and in prayers.

   ➢ Apostles and the apostolic pushes apostolic/kingdom doctrine.

   (2) Acts 15:2
   When therefore Paul and Barnabas had no small dissension and disputation with them, they determined that Paul and Barnabas, and certain other of them, should go up to Jerusalem unto the apostles and elders about this question.

   ➢ Doctrinal issues are a foundational aspect of an apostle's ministry; they are responsible for clarifying and aligning the Body of Christ with sound biblical principles.
   ➢ This critical function of the apostle is largely missing in the Body of Christ today.

9. Types of Sent People

Apostolic: is a sent or sending mission.

(1) <u>Apostles</u>

Luke 11:49 KJV

Therefore, also said the wisdom of God, I will send them prophets and apostles, and some of them they shall slay and persecute:

- Two of the apostolic government team members (prophets and apostles).

(2) <u>Ambassadors</u>

2 Cor 5:20

Now then we are ambassadors for Christ, as though God did beseech you by us: we pray you in Christ's stead, be ye reconciled to God.

➢ Ambassadors are apostolic-kingdom representatives

(3) <u>The Body of Christ</u>

Matthew 9:38 KJV

Pray ye therefore the Lord of the harvest, that he will send forth labourers into his harvest.

➢ This is a Body's specific responsibility, to pray for apostolic help.

(4) <u>Pilgrims</u>

Hebrews 11:13 KJV

These all died in faith, not having received the promises, but having seen them afar off, and were persuaded of them, and embraced them, and confessed that they were strangers and pilgrims on the earth.

(4.1)   Sojourners

Psalm 39:12

12 Hear my prayer, O LORD, and give ear unto my cry; hold not thy peace at my tears: for I am a stranger with thee, and a sojourner, as all my fathers were.

a.  The people of old; understood that they were an apostolic called people.

Course Name:         The Great Commission
Course Number:     FAT-200
Course Objective:    Defining the one and only mission of the Body of Christ.

What is the Church's Great Commission?

    a. It is the Church's primary, mission-driven purpose.

    b. It is the spreading of the gospel-kingdom message throughout the world.

    c. It is the higher calling of every local church leader.

    d. It is the Church engaging with the community locally, nationally, and internationally, with the gospel message.

    e. It is the Church's direct command from her Leader, Jesus.

Great Commission's Specific Commands

1. Great Commission

Mark 16:15

And he said unto them, <u>Go ye</u> into all the world, and preach the gospel to every creature.

    a. A command to go and preach (gospel).
    b. The world is the church's congregation not necessarily our local assemblies.

2. Matthew 28: 19-20

<u>Go ye</u> therefore, and teach all nations, baptizing them in the name of the Father, and of the Son, and of the Holy Ghost: 20 Teaching them to observe all things whatsoever I have commanded you: and, lo, I am with you always, even unto the end of the world. Amen.

Great Commission's Objectives:

a. Make converts. (To the faith)
b. To baptize (To indoctrinate into God's word or law)
c. To make disciples. (To develop followers of Jesus)
d. Advance the Kingdom's Purpose (Insert the Kingdom at hand)
e. Infiltrate the Culture (to amalgamate with God's)

3. Apostolic Commissions

John 20: 19-23

Then the same day at evening, being the first day of the week, when the doors were shut where the disciples were assembled for fear of the Jews, came Jesus and stood in the midst, and saith unto them, Peace be unto you. 20 And when he had so said, he shewed unto them his hands and his side. Then were the disciples glad when they saw the Lord. 21 Then said Jesus to them again, Peace be unto you: as my Father hath sent me, even so send I you. 22 And when he had said this, he breathed on them, and saith unto them, receive ye the Holy Ghost: 23 Whosoever sins ye remit, they are remitted unto them; and whosoever sins ye retain, they are retained.

➢ Jesus commissions the disciples as apostolic ambassadors.

➢ They were to take the kingdom message to the world.

➢ The Great Commission's feature message is the Good News.

➢ They were to establish kingdom embassies in the places they are sent on behalf of Jesus.

4. Apostolic Activation & Works

   Acts 1:6-8

   6 When they therefore were come together, they asked of him, saying, Lord, wilt thou at this time restore again the kingdom to Israel?

   7 And he said unto them, It is not for you to know the times or the seasons, which the Father hath put in his own power.

   8 But ye shall receive power, after that the Holy Ghost is come upon you: and ye shall be witnesses unto me both in Jerusalem, and in all Judaea, and in Samaria, and unto the uttermost part of the earth.

   ➤ The Great Commission comes with the power of the Holy Spirit. It is His own apostolic power and nature that is behind Christ's and the Kingdom's works.

   ➤ The endowment (Day of Pentecost) apostolic activated the church, her people, and her kingdom purpose. Acts 2:1-4.

5. The Leader's Great Commission Priorities:

➤ Is the apostle's main vision tenant.

➤ The GC will depend on your specific apostolic calling, i.e. local, regional or international.

➤ Local leaders, such as pastors and ministry heads, should view the Great Commission in their localized region as their primary focus, with national and international outreach as secondary priorities.

➤ Apostolic leader's vision and mission statements should reflect the Great Commission.

- All vision priorities should evolve around the accomplishment of the Great Commission.

6. The Theology of Sent (The God Sent Release)

Remember:

Apostolic means being 'sent from' and 'sent to.' Yet many leaders in the Body do not know who sent them, to whom they were sent, or the what, when, where, and how of their calling. Many carry titles but lack a clear sense of apostolic purpose and direction.

- The church of Jesus has an apostolic purpose and directive.
- Your ministry, church, or business should have an apostolic direction or purpose.
- Your apostolic purpose and direction don't make you an apostolic denomination.
- Your apostolic mandate infuses your visions to a level above your limited scope.

EXAMPLE OF AN APOSTOLIC SENT PERSON, CHURCH, OR MINISTRY.

Sent by Who (Paul)

1. Galatians 1:1
   Paul, an apostle, (not of men, neither by man, but by Jesus Christ, and God the Father, who raised him from the dead.

2. 
   Acts 13: 1-4
   Now there were in the church that was at Antioch certain prophets and teachers; as Barnabas, and Simeon that was called Niger, and Lucius of

Cyrene, and Manaen, which had been brought up with Herod the tetrarch, and Saul. 2 As they ministered to the Lord, and fasted, (the who) the Holy Ghost said, separate me Barnabas and Saul for the work whereunto I have called them. 3 And when they had fasted and prayed, and laid their hands on them, they (the who) sent them away. 4 So they, being sent forth by the Holy Ghost, departed unto Seleucia; and from thence they sailed to.

- First: The Holy Spirit should always be the one to send you; your commissioning must originate from Him (Acts 13:2).

- Second: You should be released by your pastor, leader, or church through prayer and fasting.

Question: How did your apostolic release into your church, ministry, business, or other area come about? Describe your release.

_____
_____
_____
_____

### Sent to What (The Work)

Acts 13: 1-4
2 As they ministered to the Lord, and fasted, the Holy Ghost said, Separate me Barnabas and Saul for the work (the what) whereunto I have called them.

Is there a specific purpose for which you were sent to your assignment for example, the delivery ministry, evangelism, the ministry to the homeless, prophetic work, etc.? Were you sent to a specific group of people in a region or to meet a particular ministry need in a community?

Note: Jesus was sent to the "Lost Sheep of Israel"

Question    To what you are specific called to (apostolically).

_____
_____

Sent When (The Time)

> Acts 13:2

As they ministered to the Lord, and fasted, (the who) the Holy Ghost said, Separate me Barnabas and Saul for the work whereunto I have called them.

- ➢ The "time" refers to when an apostle, leader, or apostolic work is released into their assignment. Most importantly, when were *you* released both by the Holy Spirit and by the church, apostle, ministry, or leader?

- ➢ The "when" signifies the divinely appointed moment you are to go.

- ➢ A proper release at the right time activates the anointing for that specific assignment. Luke 4:21

- ➢ The 'when' is the divine timing of your release, implemented by the Holy Spirit and affirmed by your spiritual covering.

Sent Where (The Location)

> Acts 13: 47

For so hath the Lord commanded us, saying, I have set thee to be a light of the Gentiles, that thou shouldest be for salvation unto the ends of the earth.

> The 'where' answers the question of why you were sent. Your location will reveal your 'who' and 'what.' 'Where' is the locator; it provides insight into the other 'W's.

Note: To where is the question? If you can answer the where, then your basic apostolic assignment questions will be address.

What: Region _____

Influence _____

Local _____

National _____

International _____

Student's Theology of Sent (The God Sent Release)

My Sent_____
       Your, organization, ministry, church, or business name

a. Sent by Who

   Question: Who is your apostolic assignment, your church home base, your apostle, pastor, or leader.

   _____
   _____

b. Sent to What

Question: To what are you specifically called to (apostolically).

_____
_____

What influence you possess for the assignment_____

What region _____

What Location _____

Spiritual Warfare in that region _____

Ministry assigned for that region_____

What specific anointing have you been given for this assignment? _____

_____

c. Sent When

Question: Who released you to your apostolic or prophetic ministry? When?

_____
_____

1. When did you receive your prophetic word concerning your release?
   _____

2. When did you receive your covering release (pastor or leader's)?
   _____

3. What is the start time of the "work"? _____

7. Student's Theology of Sent (The God Sent Release)

   d. Sent Where

   Question: To where is the question? If you can answer where; then your basic apostolic questions of your assignment will be addressed.

   _____

   _____

   What: Region _____

   Influence _____

   Local _____

   National _____

   International _____

Sent Questions: For the Office of the Apostle

1. What is your strong suit (anointing) _____?

2. What doctrinal subject (s) is your teaching strength? _____

   _____

3. What publications, books, or workbooks you have published? _____
_____

4. For what purpose where you license, ordained, or commissioned as an apostle?

_____

_____

_____

5. How many spiritual sons and daughters have you birthed? Explained your process of birthing?

_____

_____

6. How did you discover your calling? _____
_____

7. List your ministry positions you have held _____
_____

8. Explain why you believe you are called to the office of apostle or a shift to the apostolic? _____
_____

Course Name: The Apostolic Government
Course Number: FAT-300
Course Objective: To properly understand New Testament apostolic governance.

Scripture Focus: I Corinthians 12: 28

And God has appointed these in the church: first apostles, second prophets, third teachers, after that miracle, then gifts of healings, helps, administrations, varieties of tongues.

1. First:

    a. First in the Greek language is "Protos"
    b. 1) first in time or place
    c. a) in any succession of things or persons
    d. 2) first in rank
    e. a) influence, honour
    f. a) chief
    g. a) principal
    h. God has established the apostolic government order for the operation of the church.

2. Benefits of an Apostolic Government

    a. Unity for the Body of Christ and the accomplishing of the Great Commission.
    b. Cross-line Relationships
    c. Networking of resources: people, property, and apostolic principles.
    d. Foundational guidance for church and kingdom building.
    e. Nucleus for fathering and building the family of God.
    f. Wise Master Builders: People in the kingdom that are always seeing and developing paradigms, plans, visions, and articulating the foundational principles of the kingdom.

## TRUE APOSTOLIC LEADERSHIP

    a. Apostolic governance is not based on hierarchy. Rather, the most important positions of responsibility require true apostolic leaders. Apostles and apostolic leaders are not called to lord over God's people; they are called to serve.

    b. Apostolic oversight is rooted in both relationship and mission. You cannot establish biblical apostolic leadership without relationship being at its core.

3. Apostolic Leadership is:

> "A servant ministry or sent individual is called to provide godly service on behalf of the Kingdom of Heaven"

Mark 9:
33 Then He came to Capernaum. And when He was in the house He asked them, "What was it you disputed among yourselves on the road?" 34 But they kept silent, for on the road they had disputed among themselves who would be the greatest. 35 And He sat down, called the twelve, and said to them, "If anyone desires to be first, he shall be last of all and servant of all."

- This Scripture addresses the apostles (the Twelve), not general disciples.
- *Proton* (meaning "first") reminds us that godly leaders are servants; it's embedded in their spiritual DNA.

Mark chapter 6 and 12 the disciples were sent on their apostolic mission.

Apostolic principles of Serving:

    a.    Pastor    You are there for the people, to feed them spiritual milk. Acts 20:28, 2Pet 5:2

- b. Leadership — Serves the people, serves kingdom leadership in support roles.

- c. Apostle — Serves the pastor with fathering, apostolic and prophetic oversight. Acts 15:2-4, Acts 20, Rom 1:5, 1Cor 12:28

- d. Apostolic — Serves the Body of Christ as the energy and resources for the GC. Matt 28:16-20

4. Gentile Leadership Example: THE EMPHASIS ON BEING SERVED.

Mark 10:
42 But Jesus called them to Himself and said to them, "You know that those who are considered rulers over the Gentiles lord it over them, and their great ones exercise authority over them. 43 Yet it shall not be so among you; but whoever desires to become great among you shall be your servant.

Lordship: Greek 2634 kat-ak-oo-ree-yoo-o; to lord against, i.e. control, subjugate; -- exercise dominion over, over, overcome

- ➢ To "lord over" or control people is in direct opposition to the apostolic spirit.
- ➢ This kind of control has no place among apostolic leadership.
- ➢ The Body of Christ is modeled after a family: God as Father, Jesus as Son, and believers as His children.

- ➢ Apostles serve as delegated spiritual fathers based on relationship to those who willingly submit to their apostolic authority.

Gentile Leadership Principles of Serving are:

- a. Their leaders do less.
- b. Have many attendants serving their needs and desires.
- c. Intimate inept.
- d. Are often disconnected with their subordinates needs or concerns.

e. Stymies growth and production.

f. It often operates on the 'good ol' boy' system, with little to no individual development of one's gifts.

## APOSTOLIC GOVERNMENT (Church)
### An Influential Leadership Flow

### Apostle

The apostolic leader is a pioneer and strategist, setting and teaching foundational principles, while establishing doctrine. They foresee the spiritual battlefield, activate commanders, gifts, and callings, and provide future battle plans with both international and national coverage. They plan for future challenges and serve alongside the prophet for the advancement of the apostolic Body.

### Prophet

The prophet serves as the eyes of the apostolic government, foreseeing the spiritual battlefield, activating commanders, leaders, gifts, and callings. They see and guide future assignments, serving in tandem with the apostle in governance.

### Teacher

Teaches and trains the apostolic Body, with a specific focus on preparing for the Great Commission. Provides international and national coverage, instructing how to wage spiritual warfare. Serves the Body as a revelatory, anointed teacher—teaching line by line.

### Apostolic Companies

The church's small groups, developed into apostolic teams, consist of 2–3 prophets, intercessors, and apostolic members, led by a pastor with a pastoral calling. Their target is the neighborhood and broader community—bringing the church into the homes, marketplace, and local areas.

## Ministering Gifts Responsibilities Within Apostolic Body

| Apostle | Prophet | Evangelist | Pastor | Teacher |
|---|---|---|---|---|
| Foundation Specialist | Territorial Activations Seer | Body's Recruiter | Flock Care, Feeding Developing | Teaches Principles and line by line Precepts |
| Regional AP | House PR | | Local Covering | Trainer |

Note:
1. The above listed positions are from selected people who have served in five-fold gift/offices positions in the church.
2. The 1Corinthians 12:28 positions; The roles of apostles, prophets, and teachers are appointed and promoted by the Holy Spirit.
3. They are further released by apostolic leadership, oversight person, or committee.
4. The other two (Evangelist and Pastor) should be prophetic assigned and release.

Thought: They are servants that were promoted to another servant position.

Apostolic Leadership Attributes

➢ Apostolic leadership is not built on a traditional hierarchy.

➢ Apostolic leadership is built on relationships.

➢ Apostolic leaders are servants first and by nature.

➢ You can tell true bred apostolic leadership by their wiliness to serve those they lead.

➢ Apostolic leadership structure operates in influence.

What is Influence!

Definition of Influence: To earn one's confidence and trust that allows you to speak into the receiver's life.

Question: Why do you believe influence is important to an apostle or apostolic?

_____

_____

"Influence is the apostolic's power"

Course Name:	Faith Imperative
Course Number:	FAT-400
Course Objective:	Understanding the importance of faith to the apostle and the call.

Scope: The role of the apostle and the apostolic movement requires unwavering faith. It involves signs, wonders, miracles, healings, and apostolic insight often requiring you to perceive what others cannot see. As an apostle or within an apostolic environment, you will frequently be called to lead both leaders and laity into places they do not understand or cannot yet envision.

The office of the apostle and apostolic ministry will face significant opposition from both Satan and man. Moreover, strong faith is required to manifest the signs and miracles uniquely needed for this time.

Challenges to the Apostolic Transition

    a.    Traditional Church leaders and laity.

    b.    Resistance to Change

    c.    Localized Spiritual Warfare (territorial demons).

    d.    An Elongated Campaign; the vision, progress, and Christ's return (end-time closure) (the people cannot see or have patience).

    e.    Lack of Knowledge

1. Not just have it, Must live by It!
   Habakkuk 2: 4 "Behold the proud, His soul is not upright in him; But the just shall live by his faith.

   - Apostolic leader's life must be a life of faith (the apostolic cannot work with less than). Luke 19:17

   - The Apostolic ministry operates on higher levels and traverses various territories.

   - The proud will never achieve true apostolic function.

       a.    Apostolic People… Must transcend their personal faiths and beliefs. 1 Cor 4:2

  b. Apostolic People… Faith must envision multi-culture denominational operation systems. Gal 3:9

  c. Apostolic People… Faith must hold fast and conform to the Word of God. Eph 6:21, Col 1:2, 2 Tim 2:2

2. Faith must be in the power of God

   1 Corinthians 2: 1-5

   And I, brethren, when I came to you, did not come with excellence of speech or of wisdom declaring to you the testimony of God. 2 For I determined not to know anything among you except Jesus Christ and Him crucified. 3 I was with you in weakness, in fear, and in much trembling. 4 And my speech and my preaching were not with persuasive words of human wisdom, but in demonstration of the Spirit and of power, 5 that your faith should not be in the wisdom of men but in the power of God.

   ➢ The apostle Paul reveals his power source as faith in the power of God.

   ➢ Apostolic leaders walk in humility, not using their gifts for self-gratification. Acts 20:19, 1 Pet 5:8

   ➢ Like Paul, our faith must be in God's power. Mark 11:2

   ➢ It takes our faith in God, to release His apostolic will and power through us. Eph 2:8-10, Rom 4;16

3. Saving Faith (resolute faith) One's Personal faith

   ➢ Saving faith is built on rest, faith, reliance, and wholly trusting in Jesus. Wholly: entirely, totally, altogether; quiet. (Dictionary.com)

   ➢ Saving faith is more than an intellectual acknowledgment that God exists

> Saving Faith is whole heartily believing and living in faith.

Psalm 37: 3 Trust in the Lord, and do good: Dwell in the land, and feed on His faithfulness.

Proverbs 3:

5 Trust in the Lord with all your heart and lean not on your own understanding; 6 In all your ways acknowledge Him, And He shall direct your paths.

Job 5:

8 "But as for me, I would seek God, And to God I would commit my cause—

Mark 11:

22 So Jesus answered and said to them, "Have faith in God".

Benefits of "Saving Faith" for the Apostolic

a. Total reliance on Jesus for fulfilling the Great Commission.

b. Essential for the apostolic ministry's accompanying signs, wonders, and miracles.

c. A steadfast attitude of trusting the Holy Spirit for apostolic insight and guidance.

Apostolic Faith Checkup!

1. Do you believe God for tithing? _____

2. Is tithing for the New Testament Believer _____
   Explain: _____
   _____
   _____

3. Are all the gifts and fruits of the Holy Spirit relevant and active in today's church?

   Yes _____ No _____

   Explain: _____
   _____
   _____
   _____

4. What is your perception of the gift and operation of prophecy?

   Explain: _____
   _____
   _____

5. Describe what you believe about the role and office of an apostle?

   Explain: _____
   _____
   _____
   _____

6. Describe what you believe and understand about the kingdom?

   Explain: _____
   _____
   _____
   _____

7. What are your beliefs concerning the "Rapture of the Church"?

   Explain: _____
   _____
   _____
   _____

8. Is apostolic relevant for today's church?

   Explain: _____
   _____
   _____

"Your attitude will determine your altitude"
John Maxwell

Course Name: False Apostles
Course Number: FAT-500
Course Objective: Defining false leaders and avoiding pitfalls.

Foreword:

Unfortunately, many title-bearing ministers in the church today have received their ministries and offices improperly. As a result, numerous individuals are operating without the necessary knowledge, training, or wisdom, ultimately leading the Body of Christ without proper guidance.

1. Signs of a false apostle.

a. Love of Money

1 Timothy 6:10

10 For the love of money is the root of all evil: which while some coveted after, they have erred from the faith and pierced themselves through with many sorrows.

Err = Ap-op-lan-ah-o (Strong's Concordance)

Apo = from: To lead astray, to stray, (from truth) err, (going astray, going the wrong way).

Note (1):

The love of money is extremely dangerous for apostolic people ("sent ones"), as it can lead them to stray from their God-given direction. This misalignment is contrary to the apostolic calling and can result in a serious spiritual detour.

b. False Doctrines Are:
   1. Erroneous Doctrines Mark 7:7
   2. Religious Operational Paradigms 2 Pet 2:1
   3. Messages that denies scripture truths. 2 Cor 11:4, Gal 1:6-7,9, 1 Tim 4;1

   **1.** What false teachers teach will not unlock the principles in God's word.

2. The false prophet's example will be opposed to Jesus' example.

c. They Manifest False Fruit

Note (2):
There are many in ministry who are known primarily by their title or position, and this sets a poor precedent. It's like saying "tree pear" or "tree apple" instead of "pear tree" or "apple tree." The fruit identifies the tree, the tree doesn't identify itself. In the same way, it is the spiritual fruit that should authenticate the minister, not merely their title.

➢ The root issue with false leaders: their tree authenticates them. Matt 7:15

Matthew 7: 15-21
15 Beware of false prophets, which come to you in sheep's clothing, but inwardly they are ravening wolves. 16 Ye shall know them by their fruits. Do men gather grapes of thorns, or figs of thistles? 17 Even so every good tree bringeth forth good fruit; but a corrupt tree bringeth forth evil fruit. 18 A good tree cannot bring forth evil fruit, neither can a corrupt tree bring forth good fruit. 19 Every tree that bringeth not forth good fruit is hewn down and cast into the fire. 20 Wherefore by their fruits ye shall know them. 21 Not everyone that saith unto me, Lord, Lord, shall enter into the kingdom of heaven; but he that doeth the will of my Father which is in heaven.

Ravening Wolves: Gr: har-pax (727) extortion

Thorns Gr: (173) Ak-mane (acme) a point and meaning the same.

Thistles (Gr: trib-ol-os) (5148) Tribulations

➢ Apostles and apostolic people should possess and produce authentic apostolic fruit.

➢ Apostolic ministries should be "known" by its fruit.

➢ Apostolic fruit shall always correspond with the will and word of God.

- False leaders are extortionists.

- False leaders work, fruits, and presence manifest three times the trouble (tribulation).

Manifestations of False Fruits

1. Errant Followers.   Matt 15:8, 2 Tim 3:6

2. Deficient Leaders.   Acts 20:29-31, Luke 6:39, Matt 15:1-15

3. False Church and Ministries.

4. Erroneous sermons, lessons, and messages. Acts 20:29-31

5. Erroneous interpretation of Biblical Principles. Matt 15:3,16:2, Matt 23

6. False Prophecy. Jer 5:31, 29:9

7. Lies. 1 Tim 4:2

e.  They are Deceptive

Matthew 24:24
For there shall arise false Christs, and false prophets, and shall shew great signs and wonders; insomuch that, if it were possible, they shall deceive the very elect.

Deceive in the Greek language is:

Plä-nä'-ō (4105)

1) to cause to stray, to lead astray, lead aside from the right way

a) to go astray, wander, roam about

2) metaph.

a) to lead away from the truth, to lead into error, to deceive

➤ False prophets or leaders often emphasize signs and wonders, using them as evidence of their approval or legitimacy.

1) They are leaders without substance in truth or character. 1 Cor 11:18-19
2) The false prophet's ministry or ministering fails to point to Jesus.
   2 Cor 3;4, Gal 1:7-9

➤ Some of the fruit of the false is <u>departing fruit</u>:
1) People
2) Vision
3) Property declination
4) Lack of authority, he submits to no one.
5) No Break Throughs
6) Demonic Strongholds
7) Relationship Attacks
8) Disunity

d. They are Seducer

Mark 13:22
22 For false Christs and false prophets shall rise, and shall shew signs and wonders, to seduce, if it were possible, even the elect.
*Seduce= apoplanaō, meaning   apo= from. sent*
1) to cause to go astray
2) to lead away from the truth to error
3) to go astray, stray away from

e. Imposter

2 Cor 11:13-15

13 For such are false apostles, deceitful workers, transforming themselves into the apostles of Christ. 14 And no marvel; for Satan himself is transformed into an angel of light. 15 Therefore it is no great thing if his ministers also be transformed as the ministers of righteousness; whose end shall be according to their works.

Thayer's Lexicon

To transform one's self into someone, to assume one's appearance.

Imposter's False Works

- Main subject is not Jesus.

- Do not produce spiritual fruit, it produces personal fruit. Gal 1:7-9

- Their gospel doesn't match the Bible's gospel.

- Robbers of the Body, not servants, refuse to work.

- Glory seekers. Matt 6:1-2, 2 Cor 11:18

f. False Fronts

2 Peter 2: 1-3

But there were false prophets also among the people, even as there shall be false teachers among you, who privily shall bring in damnable heresies, even denying the Lord that bought them, and bring upon themselves swift destruction. 2 And many shall follow their pernicious ways; by reason of whom the way of truth shall be evil spoken of. 3 And through covetousness shall they with feigned words make merchandise of you: whose judgment now of a long time lingereth not, and their damnation slumbereth not.

1. 1. Privily: 1) to introduce or bring in secretly or craftily
   Thought:     have just a personal doctrine for you.

2. Feigned words: Greek word, (plastos1) moulded, formed, as from clay, wax, or stone; moulded, i.e. artificial or fictitious; -- feigned.

   ➢ Anyone who claims to have a unique word or doctrine and insists they alone possess this revelation, may very likely be operating in false doctrine.

Course Name:         Kingdom Unity: The Fruit of Apostolic Alignment
Course Number:       FAT-600
Course Objective:    Explore the importance of unity in the redemptive system.

Scope:      The world often sees the Body of Christ as the largest yet most divided organization on earth. The tragedy is that the Church, as a whole, does not realize how much power and influence it loses through division. If the Church is to demonstrate the power of God and be effective in winning souls, it must present a unified Body. Words may inspire, and signs and wonders may stir hearts, but without unity, a broken world will not be drawn in. The office of the Apostle and the apostolic mantle serve as catalysts for unity within the Body.

Problems with receiving the Apostolic Doctrine"

1. Many believe that the office of apostle and apostolic doctrine ended with the first-century church.

2. The vast majority of churches have adopted the culture and nature of their surrounding environments, and in doing so, have long lost the nature of Christ.

1.  The apostolic church was birth through unity.

    Act 2: 1 When the Day of Pentecost had fully come, they were all with one accord in One place.

    ➢ The apostolic church was birthed in <u>unity</u>.  Acts 2:1-4

    ➢ Unity is the <u>vital seed</u> that births the true works of God. John 17:8, 11,16-17, 21-24, Acts 4:32, Rom 15:5-6

    ➢ Apostolic unity originates from God, who empowers us to cultivate and reproduce it

2. Unity was the daily and mode of operation for the apostolic church.
Act 2: 42 So continuing daily with one accord in the temple, and breaking bread from house to house, they ate their food with gladness and simplicity of heart.

➢ Unity in people produces unity in outcome. Phil 3:16-17

➢ Unity is the base ingredient of worship, signs, wonders, and miracle ministry.

3. Apostolic decisions are conceived and birth out of unity.
Acts 15: 25 it seemed good to us, being assembled with one accord, to send chosen men to you with our beloved Barnabas and Paul.

Proverbs 11:14b
"But in the multitude of counsellors there is safety".

➢ Godly decisions should be pursued in an astrosphere of unity. Pro 1:5, 11:14, 15:22, 27:9

4. Christ: Unity's Source

John 17:
8 For I have given unto them the words which thou gavest me; and they have received them and have known surely that I came out from thee, and they have believed that thou didst send me.

10 And all mine are thine, and thine are mine; and I am glorified in them.
11 And now I am no more in the world, but these are in the world, and I come to thee. Holy Father, keep through thine own name those whom thou hast given me, that they may be one, as we are.

21  That they all may be one; as thou, Father, art in me, and I in thee, that they also may be one in us: that the world may believe that thou hast sent me

22  And the glory which thou gavest me I have given them; that they may be one, even as we are one:

23  I in them, and thou in me, that they may be made perfect in one; and that the world may

Apostolic Unity

- The word of God is a unifier; it brings the giver and receiver into relationship. Eph 4:4

- In unity, Christ is glorified; in self-serving, self is magnified.

- Under the name of God, we are unified. Eph 4:4-6, Mark 16:15-20

- Oneness expresses ultimately unity, this type of unity registers to the heart of unbelievers. John 13:35

- Perfection comes in unity with Christ, not in individual works. Eph 2:10

5. Unity in the Spirit

Romans 12:

16  Be of the same mind one toward another. Mind not high things but condescend to men of low estate. Be not wise in your own conceits.

- Apostolic people possess unity in the spirit (spiritual connection) not just in the physical or soulish realm. John 16:13-14, Eph 4:3

- The Holy Spirit is the unified God in the earth, working in the church.

6.  Apostle Unity Flow

Psalm 133:

Behold, how good and how pleasant it is for brethren to dwell together in unity! 2 It is like the precious oil upon the head, running down on the beard, The beard of Aaron, Running down on the edge of his garments. 3 It is like the dew of Hermon, descending upon the mountains of Zion; For there the Lord commanded the blessing-- Life forevermore.

- ➢ Apostolic unity is good for the Body.

- ➢ Apostolic unity flows from the head to the Body.

- ➢ Apostolic unity represents the flow of the Spirit.

Course Name:            Fellowship: The Missing Link (Fellowship)
Course Number:        FAT-700
Course Objective:      To emphasize that fellowship has been missing in the Church for years and to create a sense of urgency for this vital doctrine to be restored and reinvigorated within the Body of Christ.

Scope:                 Many times, the Body of Christ projects an attitude of being "so spiritually minded that we are of no earthly good." As a result, both the Church and the world are often turned off by us. Why? Because people, both inside and outside the Church, feel neglected due to a pious attitude and a genuine lack of fellowship.

<u>We as the people of God failed to understand fellowship is essential because</u>:

1. It's good for the soul.
2. Good for the health of man.
3. Fellowship is what the church is birthed out of.
4. People search hard for fellowship.
5. Fellowship is a major attribute of the apostolic grace.
6. Fellowship is the substance of unity.
7. It's the substance of the statement; "this is how the world will know that you're My disciples."
8. Fellowship is a fruit of salvation and a central ingredient in the family of God.

1.     WE CANNOT AFFORD TO FORGET THE IMPORTANCE OF FELLOWSHIP!

Fellowship is often undervalued in traditional church settings. In the apostolic church, however, it holds the highest urgency and importance. Without fellowship, apostolic vision loses its vitality. In the early days of the Church, fellowship was so essential that without it, the Church would have died in its infancy.

2. GOD SAID IT IS NOT GOOD! (NO FELLOWSHIP)

   2a. Genesis 2:
   18 And the Lord God said, "It is not good that man should be alone; I will make him a helper comparable to him."

   - Through <u>divine insight</u>, we understand that the absence of fellowship is harmful. Man was created for both physical <u>fellowship with others and spiritual fellowship</u> with the Father.
   - Man was ultimately created to fellowship with God their Creator.

   - Apostolic fellowship forms the foundational unit the spiritual family that initiates the birth of a church, ministry, or organization within God's divine order.

3. APOSTOLIC FELLOWSHIP

   Fellowship in the Greek language: (Koy-nohn-ee-ah)   Koinonia = fellowship.
   *Koinonia* is the anglicisation of a <u>Greek</u> word (κοινωνία) that means communion by intimate participation. From Wikipedia, the free encyclopedia

   3a. Premiere "Fellowship" Scripture

   Acts 2
   42 And they continued steadfastly in the apostles' doctrine and fellowship, in the breaking of bread, and in prayers. 43 Then fear came upon every soul, and many wonders and signs were done through the apostles. 44 Now all who believed were together, and had all things in common, 45 and sold their possessions and goods, and divided them among all, as anyone had need. 46 So continuing daily with one accord in the temple, and breaking bread from house to house, they ate their food

with gladness and simplicity of heart, 47 praising God and having favor with all the people. And the Lord added to the church daily those who were being saved.

3b. True Apostolic Fellowship Produces:

- Conducive environment for signs and wonders.
- Corporate (warring) Prayer.
- Unity.
- Lack of Selfishness.
- Fertile ground for revelation of God's word.
- Conducive environment for people growth.
- Personal spiritual growth of individual gifts and callings.

3c. Reasons Why People Join (Fellowship):

- People often come to faith out of a deep longing for fellowship with God though the reasons behind that longing may vary.

- People join the church to fellowship with other like-minded people.

- People join because they sense the connectivity in that church's fellowship.

- People join to connect their immediate family with others to fulfill human needs.

- People join seeking purpose through fellowship.

**4.** APOSTOLIC FELLOWSHIP Is:

- A. COMMUNICATION
- B. COMMUNION
- C. CONTRIBUTION
- D. COMMONALITY

4a. COMMUNICATING:
(The teaching, preaching, and spreading of the gospel through the vehicle of fellowship)

(Acts 2: 42 and they continued steadfastly in the apostles' doctrine).

> 4.1 Apostolic people share their faith.
> Philemon 1: 4 I thank my God, making mention of thee always in my prayers, 5 Hearing of thy love and faith, which thou hast toward the Lord Jesus, and toward all saints; 6 That the communication of thy faith may become effectual by the acknowledging of every good thing which is in you in Christ Jesus.

- ➤ The sharing of your faith is an active part of apostolic fellowship of the believers. 2Cor 5:20, 1Pet 3;15

- ➤ In fellowship the "new" kingdom's message is received by faith.

- ➤ It is through fellowship that the Gospel's "new faith" is communicated and received. (Romans 10:17)

4b. COMMUNION
(The partaking and sharing of the vicarious works of Jesus through the communion's elements)

4b.1   1 Corinthians 10: 16-17

16 The bread which we break, is it not the communion of the body of Christ? 17 For we, though many, are one bread and one body; for we all partake of that one bread.

> Communion brings the Body into the apostolic mode. Gal 4:6, Acts 2:42

> For believers, the communion ceremony is more than a ritual, it is a sacred time of fellowship with Jesus. 1Cor 10:16-17, 1John 1:3

> The communion with Jesus is the nucleus of all Christian fellowships. 2Cor 6:16, 2Cor 13:14

4b.2   <u>Communion is designed to bring us together in several ways:</u>

a. With Christ and one another. Psa16:7, Phil 2:1-2, 1TH 5:11,14

b. In Christ (a baptism into His teachings, life). Eph 4:4-5, Gal 3;27, 1Cor 12:13

c. It brings us in compliance with the Greatest Commandment.

4b.3   Apostolic Correction for Communion Purpose

Note: While this passage of Scripture is commonly used to guide the conduct of communion services, it is an apostolic correction addressing the true purpose and meaning of communion.

1Corinthians 11:18-26

18 For first of all, when you come together as a church, I hear that there are divisions among you, and in part I believe it. 19 For there must also be factions among you, that those who are approved may be recognized among you. 20 Therefore when you come together in one place, it is not to eat the Lord's Supper. 21 For in eating, each one takes his own supper ahead of others; and one is hungry and another is drunk. 22 What! Do you not have houses to eat and drink in? Or do you despise the church of God and shame those who have nothing? What shall I say to you? Shall I praise you in this? I do not praise you. 23 For I received from the Lord that which I also delivered to you: that the Lord Jesus on the same night in which He was betrayed took bread; 24 and when He had given thanks, He broke it and said, "Take, eat; this is My body which is broken for you; do this in remembrance of Me." 25 In the same manner He also took the cup after supper, saying, "This cup is the new covenant in My blood. This do, as often as you drink it, in remembrance of Me." 26 For as often as you eat this bread and drink this cup, you proclaim the Lord's death till He comes.

Paul's Apostolic Communion "Correction Issues"

➢ Their communion failed to bring "unity."

➢ Religious communions produce factions (sectarian) division and are a threat to apostolic communion connection (fellowship).

➢ They partook ahead of others: The selfish act of not waiting on the others negated one the most important benefits of communion "unity".

➢ A proper communion celebration always focuses on Jesus; when the communion is religious (going through the motions) it spurs personal recognition.

4c.    CONTRIBUTE

    4c.1    Equates to "One for All" Mentalities

    Acts 2:
    45 and sold their possessions and goods, and divided them among all, as anyone had need.

- Apostolic fellowship fosters apostolic community, sending a clear message to outsiders that we are united as one people.

    4c.2    Apostolic Revelation, Spurns Corporate Giving
    Romans 15
    26 For it pleased those from Macedonia and Achaia to make a certain contribution for the poor among the saints who are in Jerusalem. 27 It pleased them indeed, and they are their debtors. For if the Gentiles have been partakers of their spiritual things, their duty is also to minister to them in material things.

- Apostolic fellowship dismisses selfishness.

- True apostolic fellowship naturally cultivates a spirit of giving there is no need to beg or pressure people to give under this kind of operation and anointing. 2Cor 9:1-5

    4c.3    Apostolic Life Produces Good Works, Giving People, and Willing Spirit to Share.

    1 Timothy 6:
    17 Command those who are rich in this present age not to be haughty, nor to trust in uncertain riches but in the living God, who gives us richly all

things to enjoy. 18 Let them do good, that they be rich in good works, ready to give, willing to share.

- Apostolic ministries produce people who are willing and eager to serve.

4c.4  Sharing is Part of an Apostolic Priest Duties
Hebrews 13: 15-16

15 Therefore by Him let us continually offer the sacrifice of praise to God, that is, the fruit of our lips, giving thanks to His name. 16 But do not forget to do good and to share, for with such sacrifices God is well pleased.

4d.  COMMONALITY (share) (partnership)

Note:  In classical Greek, koinonein means "to have a share in a thing," as when two or more people hold something, or even all things, in common. (From Wikipedia, the free encyclopedia).

4d.1  Apostolic Members Share the same Spirit.

Philippians 2:

1 Therefore if there is any consolation in Christ, if any comfort of love, if any fellowship of the Spirit, if any affection and mercy,

2 fulfill my joy by being like-minded, having the same love, being of one accord of one mind.

3 Let nothing be done through selfish ambition or conceit, but in lowliness of mind let each esteem others better than himself.

4 Let each of you look out not only for his own interests, but also for the interests of others.

5 Let this mind be in you which was also in Christ Jesus.

- A proper attitude toward communion positions the hearts and minds of participants to be in one accord spiritually. Gal 4:6, 1Cor 12:12-13

4d.2    The Apostolic Body Shares the same Drink

1 Corinthians13

13 For by one Spirit we were all baptized into one body--whether Jews or Greeks, whether slaves or free--and have all been made to drink into one Spirit. 14 For in fact the body is not one member but many.

- Apostolic believers are common and are one in the Body of Christ. 1Cor 12: 12-13, Eph 4:1-3

4d.3    Considering and Stirring Love in One Another

Hebrews 10:

24 And let us consider one another in order to stir up love and good works, 25 not forsaking the assembling of ourselves together, as is the manner of some, but exhorting one another, and so much the more as you see the Day approaching.

Course Name: Apostolic Company
Course Number: FAT-800
Course Objective: Construct and reform traditional church settings into biblically sound apostolic companies.

Scope:
a. The goal of the apostolic company is to create a vibrant environment where members of the local church can grow, develop, and actively use their spiritual gifts and callings.

b. The primary purpose of the apostolic company is to serve as an extension of the local pastoral ministry.

c. Its major function is to care for people beyond the four walls of the church within its sphere of influence on behalf of the Kingdom, the church, and the pastor.

Apostolic Function:

1. To assist the church in transitioning into a fully functioning apostolic body.

2. To effectively meet both the spiritual and practical needs of the surrounding community.

3. To actively fulfill the Great Commission and all of its related responsibilities.

Apostolic Company Challenges:

1. Current leadership is often unwilling to relinquish control.
2. A lack of desire among leaders to move beyond traditional church models.
3. Difficulty in discerning the voice and leading of the Holy Spirit.
4. Limited understanding of apostolic and Kingdom principles.

5. Leaders and members have been shaped by traditional church paradigms.
6. Fear of launching a new work during their leadership tenure.
7. Concern over losing influence or control.
8. Negative examples and past abuses associated with the apostolic office and ministry.

1. Definition of Apostolic Company

    1a. It is a component of the apostolic church that functions like a subdivision, neighborhood, community, or city hub, where members gather for fellowship and worship within their local area, typically during mid-week services.

    1b. Leadership teams and members consist of five-fold ministers and members that are in that same geographical location.

    1c. Its local members are that apostolic company's nucleus.

2. Example of an apostolic church:

    2a. Exodus 18:
    21 Moreover you shall select from all the people able men, such as fear God, men of truth, hating covetousness; and place such over them to be rulers of thousands, rulers of hundreds, rulers of fifties, and rulers of tens.

    Example: A church with one thousand members is divided into ten apostolic communities, each consisting of one hundred members, and designated as an apostolic company.

    2b. Mark 6:
    39 Then He commanded them to make them all sit down in groups on the green grass. 40 So they sat down in ranks, in hundreds and in fifties

3. Apostolic Company's Mission:

   ➢ To provide an adequate training ground for the members to exercise their gifts and callings.

   ➢ To provide adequate training environments for apostolic five-fold leaders.

   ➢ To provide more laborers for the field of harvest (apostolic community), Great Commission, and assigned regions.

   ➢ To provide an open Heaven for the company's assignment.

   ➢ To provide an open Heaven for signs and wonders in the community.

   ➢ To activate a Market Place ministry and anointing in the assigned community.

4. Apostolic Company Leadership and Membership Configuration
   (company/team configuration)

   4.1  A company consists of 50-100 (more or less) family members or singles in a particular community, subdivision, or region. The group is led by a pastor/deacon member with a *pastoral* calling or gift.

   4.2  An apostolic company's structure consists of an Apostolic Team, Prophetic Team, Prayer Team and Members.

4a. Apostolic Team (part of the apostolic team of the Apostolic Company.)
   ➢ Consists of 2-3 five-fold ministers with apostolic training to minister to the people, within an apostolic company.

4b. Prophetic Team (part of the apostolic team of the Apostolic Company.)

- Always operate and under the tutelage of the church's House Prophet.
- Team consists of two-three prophets.
- The team works in conjunction with AP and prayer team.
- Realistic and strictly guided prophets in training programs.

4c. Prayer Team (warfare) (part of the apostolic team of the Apostolic Company.)
- It consists of 2-3 members per team.
- Under the tutelage of the church's corporate prayer leader.
- Prayer focus (mainly) on the apostolic company assigned to.
- Prays for the team and community's needs.

4d. Membership (part Apostolic Company.)
- It consists of the members that physically live or reside in that geographical location.
- Ultimately, the membership belongs to the church (under senior pastor's care),
- The members/apostolic company operate under the small group ministry concept.

4e. Team Responsibilities:
- The Apostolic Team Members teaches, preach, and minister apostolic, kingdom, and biblical doctrine to their assigned areas.
- The Prophetic Team Members prophesy, teaches and preach to their assigned areas.
- The Prayer Team Members pray, lead in corporate prayer, and assist in prophetic ministry to the assigned area.
- The membership fellowships with one another and share their faith in their community.

Notes:

1. An apostolic team's core can consist of an apostolic, prophetic, and prayer members.
2. An apostolic company's designs are for the propagating of the Great Commission.
3. Reaching the community and the developing of the Body's grace gifts.

**5.** Church Composition within Apostolic Companies
   1. 1000 member church.
   2. Senior Pastor as the leader.

5a. Inner-Core Leaders: (the leaders that are the closest to the pastor)

   1. Executive Pastor
   2. Associate Pastor (House Prophet?)
   3. Elder: family Ministry/Care

Notes:

1. The actual positions responsibilities could vary depending on vision and pastorate; nevertheless, senior leaders should be holding the leadership positions of his/her inner core.

2. Pastoral positions (apostolic company leaders) should be given to those who have pastoral calling and experience (for the protection of the people and membership).

3. If you do not have senior, seasoned leaders, do not feel obligated to fill that position now. Wait on the Holy Spirit and the seasoning of your leadership core.

5b.   Outer Court Leaders and Administrative Leaders

| Five-Fold Ministry | Administrative Church Leaders |
|---|---|
| Apostle | Bishop |
| Prophet | Elder |
| Evangelist | Teacher |
| Pastor | Preacher |
| Teacher | Superintendent |
|  | Deacon |
|  | Auxiliary Leaders |

Note:   Under the auspices of apostolic order, the five-fold ministry is the set group for the perfecting and edifying of the Body. Eph 4:11

6.   Apostolic Company Overview (EXAMPLE)

1. 100 members: Rose Garden Subdivision
2. (group leader) elder/pastoral called leaders/deacon.
3. Apostolic team (5-fold ministry) consists of apostolic team from within.
4. Prophetic team (prophetic leaders under the guidance of house prophet). Consists of members within.
5. Prayer Team consisting of 2-3 members. Consists of members within.
6. 100-member group of people that reside in that subdivision, neighborhood, community or city.

Notes:

1. An apostolic company (100-member team) is one of the church's areas or communities that belongs to the 1000-member church.

2. The leader of each apostolic company must possess a pastoral calling.

3. The example above would be one of ten companies designated in this 1000-member church.

4. The apostolic company best serves to take care of all of the people needs, to take neighborhoods, communities, and regions with your vision and localized Great Commission.

5. The apostolic company best serves to develop, train, and permit the members to flow and develop in their individual gifts.

Apostolic Company Meeting Itinerary

Apostolic Company's families are divided up into geographically assignments. Families meet once a week in (preferably) different homes or suitable facilities in that community. An apostolic company leader leads the company, and a family host the group meeting.

Apostolic Company Motto:    People Care & People Connection

Apostolic Company's Purpose:

1. To take the gospel of Jesus Christ into the community and marketplace.

2. Provide a more intimate environment conducive for a God connection.

3. The create an environment more individualized for Family and Individuals spiritual needs.

4. Connection with others: Fellowship

5. Community Corporate Prayer

<u>Not AP Company's Objective</u>:

    a.    To Be a Church or Ministry.

    b.    To Promote One's Ambitions.

    c.    Denominationalism

    d.    Community Social Club: See number 4 above.

    e.    Traditionalism

    f.    Sectarian, Faction, or Clique Behavior.

Company's Worship Format:

Welcome-    7:00-7:20pm.  (Pastor/Leader)

- It is a time of warming up to each other and refreshments are served.
- Connecting with different families and members.
- Connecting with other skill members that can help their fellow members.

Worship-    7:20-7:30pm  (Prophetic and Prayer Team)

- Is focusing on and blessing God with our praises, exercising the gifts of the Holy Spirit, to encourage, and build up the apostolic company. Apostolic and prophetic team members assist the leader.

Word- (lesson)    7:30-7:50pm.  (Pastor/Leader)

- Is applying God's Word in order to transform the way we live our lives. We revisit the word that was taught on the previous Sunday (worship service).

Works-  7:30-7:50pm.  (Pastor, Prophetic, and Prayer)

- ➢ Is praying for the unsaved in our community, families and friends; also planning for the next evangelistic outreach and doing good works. The prayer team leads and assists in individual prayer requests.

Group Keys:

1. This group operates in the community.
2. More members' are developed and use their gifts in this type of setting.
3. Membership actively involved in ministry in the community.
4. Potential senior and five-fold leaders are discovered and developed.
5. Evangelism is a high priority.
6. Active concerning ministry in the community.
7. More visible presence of Christ in the community.
8. Goal is to take the community for Christ.

Course Name: Building Apostolic and Prophetic Teams
Course Number: FAT-900
Course Objective: To discuss how to develop the gifts and teams for the apostolic church.

Scope:

1. Many gifted and talented saints remain inactive in the church, simply observing a few prominent individuals consistently operating in their gifts, while their own potential remains undeveloped.

2. The integration of apostolic and prophetic teams within the church and apostolic companies creates greater opportunities for individuals to be equipped, developed, and released in their spiritual gifts.

Note: Both teams will remain under the ongoing guidance and mentorship of the house prophet and apostolic leader. This structure ensures safety, accountability, and effective development for both the team members and the local Body

Guidelines for Establishing Apostolic and Prophetic Programs:

a. The apostolic and prophetic programs must be established under the direction of the local pastor or church leader.

b. Through prayer and fasting, the pastor should appoint a House Prophet to oversee the training and development of the church's prophetic core.

c. Similarly, through prayer and fasting, the pastor should appoint a House Apostolic Leader/Trainer to lead and train the apostolic core.

d. In collaboration with the House Prophet and the House Apostolic Leader, the pastor should engage in prayer and fasting to develop comprehensive training programs for both teams.

Team's Objectives:

a. Foster an environment that supports the development and activation of each member's spiritual gifts.

b. Create a healthy atmosphere where members can operate in and be trained in their gifts.

c. Extend the use of these gifts beyond the four walls of the church, reaching into the community from the sanctuary to the street corners.

1. Apostolic Team Training Agenda

- Successfully complete the F.A.T. Course or an equivalent apostolic training program.
- Complete an Apostolic Leadership Training Course (advanced leadership development).
- Complete the DEJ Ministry Basic Leadership Course or an approved equivalent.
- Complete the DEJM Apostolic-Kingdom Course or a comparable course.
- Participate in Team Assignments (ongoing practical training).
- Engage in Team Training Sessions (ongoing development).

2. Prophetic Team Training Agenda

- The House Prophet shall develop a training outline for the team, including a minimum of six hours of classroom instruction.
- The House Prophet shall schedule dates and times for practical training, including altar ministry, corporate prayer, and other ministry opportunities.
- Develop an individual counseling program for prophets-in-training

- ➤ Team Assignments.
- ➤ Team Training.

3. Prayer Team Training Agenda

   Actively serve as members of the church/ministry's Corporate Prayer Team.

   Complete Prayer and Warfare Prayer Training Sessions (held annually).

   Complete the DEJ Ministry Basic Leadership Course or an approved equivalent.

   Complete the F.A.T. Course or an equivalent foundational training program.

   Participate in Basic Prophetic Training, with an annual refresher recommended.

1. Teams Weekly Agenda

    1. Serve in altar ministry as part of corporate ministry.

    2. Participate regularly in corporate prayers.

    3. Assist with salvation and rededication ministry during altar ministry.

    4. Serve within an apostolic company assigned to a community (assigned by the House Prophet and Apostolic Leader).

    5. Attend periodic leadership development meetings and training sessions.

    6. Attend periodic ministry development meetings (apostolic or prophetic).).

2. Practical Team Training Outline

   5A. HOW DO YOU ESTABLISH AN APOSTOLIC TEAM

   1. APOSTOLIC TEAMS MEMBERS ARE FIVE-FOLD MINISTERS.
   2. THEY SHOULD HAVE AT LEAST 2 YEARS OF TRAINING.
   3. THEY SHOULD HAVE COMPLETED A CHRISTIAN LEADERSHIP COURSE.
   4. NEED TO BE LICENSE AND OR ORDAINED.

   5B. BIBLICAL STANDARD FOR TEAM/MINISTRY SEPRATION
   ACTS 13:
   1 Now in the church that was at Antioch there were certain prophets and teachers: Barnabas, Simeon who was called Niger, Lucius of Cyrene, Manaen who had been brought up with Herod the tetrarch, and Saul. 2 As they ministered to the Lord and fasted, the Holy Spirit said, "Now separate to Me Barnabas and Saul for the work to which I have called them." 3 Then, having fasted and prayed, and laid hands on them, they sent them away.

   ➤ The apostle and apostolic is a God (only) called task.

   ➤ The revelation about teams and members shall be sought through prayer and fasting. Acts 6:6, 13:3

   ➤ You are not released because you have a calling, your church after fasting and prayer releases you, as the Holy Spirit commands. ACTS 13:2,4, 9:15

6. HOW DO YOU ESTABLISH AN PROPHETIC TEAM

1. Must have a prophetic calling—this includes:

- Called to the office of the prophet
- Functioning as a seer
- Operating in the gift of prophecy
- Receiving prophetic dreams or visions

2. Must have completed or be actively completing a Basic Leadership Course.

3. Must be a member of the local church.

Apostolic: Recommended Apostolic Reading & Training Resource

A Shift in Leadership          John Eckhardt

Apostolic Ministry             John Kelly

Apostles The fathering Servant Bill Scheidler


Prophetic: Recommended Apostolic Reading & Training Resource

Prophets and the Prophetic Movement    Dr. Bill Hamon

Prophets Pitfalls and Principles       Dr. Bill Hamon

Prophets and personal Prophecy         Dr. Bill Hamon

Course Name: How to Properly Transition to an Apostolic Body
Course Number: FAT-1000
Course Objective: To assist the leader in transitioning his assembly from its current state into an apostolic body.

Apostolic Transition Tasks

Task 1   The pastor/leader prays and seeks God's guidance regarding the transition.

Task 2:   As God speaks, the pastor begins revamping the ministry's vision, mission, and purpose.

Task 3:   Share the God-given vision shifts with inner-core leaders only.

Task 4:   Spend 21 days in prayer and fasting with inner-core leaders to seek confirmation and unity in the new direction.

Task 5:   Present the apostolic shift to all ministry leaders. Begin apostolic leadership training with the full leadership team.

Task 6:   Announce the apostolic shift to the entire congregation. The pastor begins teaching on apostolic subjects to lay the foundation. The goal is to release apostolic knowledge, revelation, and anointing which must be both taught and spiritually "caught" by the laity.

Task 7:   Invite apostles, prophets, and apostolic teachers to assist in confirming the shift through activation, impartation, and further training.

Task 8:   Transition the Body into an apostolic teaching ministry. Continue using the ministers from Task 7 for support and instruction.

Task 9:   Begin developing apostolic communities and ministry teams. After 6 to 12 months of training, allow for supervised ministry activity.

Task 10: Establish and begin operating as apostolic companies. This includes defining their structure, restrictions, and function.

Task 11: Conduct a transition meeting with both inner- and outer-core leaders. Review all aspects of the apostolic shift and make necessary adjustments.

Course Name: Apostolic Strategy
Course Number: FAT-1100
Course Objective: To develop the leader's to see and interpret apostolic strategy and planning.

Scope:

The apostle should possess the insight to strategically position and guide the Body into alignment with the greater mission: advancing the global apostolic mandate of the Great Commission.

The Great Commission Requires:

1. Clarity of purpose understanding who is being sent, what the mission is, when and where it is to take place.

2. Confirmation through signs, wonders, and mighty deeds.
3. A ministry of healing and deliverance.

4. Faith, accompanied by apostolic strategy.

5. A sound eschatological understanding of the Body's role in alignment with the Church's fulfillment of the Great Commission.

Note: 1. If in your discerning, you are only able to see recreation, community, and outreach centers, there is a possibility you are not an apostle or you lack the proper insight. (This is a pastoral insight for a community).

2. Apostles and apostolic people develop strategy and lead the people of God into their spiritual positions and wars. The church is not some happy go lucky outfit. Remember, "The Kingdom is advancing by force."

Personal Apostolic Equipping Requirements:

1. Discernment
2. Baptism of the Holy Spirit with tongues (essential you will need for the apostolic insight).
3. The actual calling of the office of Apostle or to the apostolic.
4. Know and understand your "Who, What, When, and Where of your apostolic release.
5. Sound apostolic & kingdom revelation.

Apostolic Strategy Objectives:

1. To develop the apostle and apostolic strategy.
2. To be able to enter a church, ministry, business, or community and develop an apostolic strategy for them.
3. To provide apostolic guidance to all within your realm of influence.
4. To provide a hard copy of the specific strategy to the leader.

Warfare- Strategy

1a. Strategy Define:

Note: Vine's Expository Dictionary
4754: strateuomai // strateuomai // strat-yoo'-om-ahee // middle voice from the base of 4756 ; TDNT - 7:701,1091; v, AV - war 5, goeth a warfare 1, soldier 1; 7
1) to make a military expedition, to lead soldiers to war or to battle, (spoken of a commander). 2) to do military duty, be on active service, be a soldier. 3) to fight

- ✓ One of the primary responsibilities of an apostle is to lead their assignments into spiritual formation and spiritual warfare (see 1 Corinthians 1:1; 1 Corinthians 16:24; Acts 15).

- ✓ The office of the apostle is designed to provide strategic direction to those with whom they are in a relationship.

- ✓ Apostles and apostolic teams engage in spiritual battles against opposing forces.

1b. Heavenly Military Call

> Hebrews 3:1
> Therefore, holy brethren, partakers of the heavenly calling, consider the Apostle and High Priest of our confession, Christ Jesus,

    a. Jesus is the Apostle and High Priest of our faith.

    b. Jesus' earthly ministry demonstrated apostolic power, authority, and nurturing (maternal) characteristics.

    c. The office of the apostle and apostolic ministry originate from Jesus, the Chief Apostle

1c. Jesus as Captain of the Salvation (Army).

> Hebrews 2: 9-10
> 9 But we see Jesus, who was made a little lower than the angels, for the suffering of death crowned with glory and honor, that He, by the grace of God, might taste death for everyone. 10 For it was fitting for Him, for whom are all things and by whom are all things, in bringing many sons to glory, to make the captain of their salvation perfect through sufferings.

- ✓ It is a fact that the Body of Christ has been engaged in spiritual warfare since the entrance of sin into the world.

2. Military Orders

Note: In every type of operation, whether business, military, administrative, or spiritual warfare—orders and directives must be both given and received.

2a. Military Occupation (warfare, strategy)

Luke 19:12

He said therefore, a certain nobleman went into a far country to receive for himself a kingdom, and to return. 13 And he called his ten servants, and delivered them ten pounds, and said unto them, Occupy till I come.

Occupy is a business and military term.

- ✓ In this particular scripture, the term "occupy" refers to conducting business transactions.

- ✓ However, when viewed through a military lens—as seen in Luke 19 "occupy" also carries an apostolic perspective. It implies both taking territory and conducting business on behalf of the apostolic Kingdom mandate.

Apostolic Occupation Business:

a. To engage in apostolic work and trade (focused on advancing the Kingdom).

b. Make disciples as a central aspect of apostolic mission.

c. Act as ambassadors of the Kingdom, representing the government of God on earth.

d. Conduct Kingdom business, ensuring the establishment and expansion of God's rule.

e. Occupy as an ambassador or Apostle General, acting on behalf of the King and His Kingdom.

2b. Jesus' Specific Battle Orders
Joel 2: 1-11

1. 1 Blow the trumpet in Zion and sound an alarm in My holy mountain! Let all the inhabitants of the land tremble; For the day of the Lord is coming, for it is at hand: 2 A Day of darkness and gloominess, A day of clouds and thick darkness, Like the morning clouds spread over the mountains. A people come, great and strong, the like of whom has never been; Nor will there ever be any such after them, even for many successive generations. 3 A fire devours before them, and behind them a flame burns; The land is like the Garden of Eden before them, and behind them a desolate wilderness; Surely nothing shall escape them. 4 Their appearance is like the appearance of horses; And like swift steeds, so they run. 5 With a noise like chariots Over mountaintops they leap, Like the noise of a flaming fire that devours the stubble, like a strong people set in battle array. 6 Before them the people writhe in pain; All faces are drained of color. 7 They run like mighty men, they climb the wall like men of war; Everyone marches in formation, and they do not break ranks. 8 They do not push one another; Everyone marches in his own column. Though they lunge between the weapons, they are not cut down. 9 They run to and fro in the city, they run on the wall; They climb into the houses, they enter at the windows like a thief. 10 The earthquakes before them, the heavens tremble; The sun and moon grow dark, And the stars diminish their brightness.

**2.** 11 The Lord gives voice before His army, For His camp is very great; For strong is the One who executes His word. For the day of the Lord is great and very terrible; Who can endure it?

- ✓ An apostolic call emanates from an apostle or apostolic person.

- ✓ The apostle or apostolic person sounds the alarm within the Body of Christ.

- ✓ "Blow the trumpet" refers to acting, working, and operating in the fruits, gifts, spirit, and other spiritual matters.

- ✓ Jesus, as the Apostolic Voice of our faith, speaks through His words and His battle cry, which becomes our voice.

2c. Apostles and Apostolic Call to Warfare

1 Timothy 1:18
This charge I commit to you, son Timothy, according to the prophecies previously made concerning you, that by them you may wage the good warfare,

➢ Paul gives Timothy an apostolic charge for war.

1. Apostolic Strategic Concept of Operations

2 Corinthians 10:
3 For though we walk in the flesh, we do not war according to the flesh. 4 For the weapons of our warfare are not carnal but mighty in God for pulling down strongholds, 5 casting down arguments and every high thing that exalts itself against the knowledge of God, bringing every thought into captivity to the obedience of Christ,

- ✓ Paul provides apostolic instruction for an apostolic offensive.

- ✓ Paul outlines specific warfare strategies, including the characteristics of weapons, tactics for attacking strongholds, targeting arguments and high places (enemy locations), and bringing the enemy into captivity (enemy arrest).

2. Apostolic (INSUM) Intelligence Summary (2Corinthians 10:3-5)

    a. Enemy Formation (we do not war according to the flesh).

    - ➤ The enemy is a spiritual force. 1Sam 16:14, 1Pet 5:8, Col 1:13, Eph 6:12, Rev 12:10

    b. Enemy's Attack Strategy (casting down arguments and every high thing that exalts itself against the knowledge of God).

    - ➤ The enemy's main attack approach is through the mind of God's Army. 1Cor 2:11, 2 Cor 4:4

3. Apostolic (OPORD)   Operation Order
   (Strategy to Wage War)

   2 Corinthians 10: 3-5 & Ephesians 6: 10-18

   a. Situation

      1. This war is not against flesh and blood (Eph 6).
      2. We war not after the flesh (it's a spiritual war (2 Cor 10)
      3. Enemy Opposing Force (s): (1) principalities, (2) powers, (3) rulers of darkness of this world (4) spiritual wickedness in high places (Eph 6).

4. To repel the fiery darts of the enemy (Eph 6).

b. Mission

1. To bring every thought into captivity to the obedience of Christ (2 Cor 10).
2. To stand (in God) in the evil days (Eph 6).
3. To watch with all perseverance and supplication for all saints (Eph 6).
4. To be strong in the Lord (Eph 6).
5. To put on the whole armor of God (Eph 6).

c. Execution

1. To pull down strongholds (Eph 6).
2. Cast down arguments (Eph 6).
3. Cast down the high places that exalt itself against God (Eph 6).

d. Service Support

1. <u>Protective Battle Gear:</u>

   a. Girt your loins with truth, Defensive Weapon (Eph 6).

   b. Breast Plate of Righteousness, Defensive Weapon (Eph 6).

   c. Foot Protection: Shod with the Gospel of Peace, Offensive Weapon (Eph 6).

   d. Overall Protection: Above all the Shield of Faith, Defensive Weapon (Eph 6).

  e. Head Protection: The Helmet of Salvation, Offensive Weapon (Eph 6).

  f. The Sword of the Spirit: Offensive Weapon (Eph 6).

e. Command
 1. Our weapons are not carnal, but mighty in God (Eph 6).
 2. Communication Channel: Praying always with all prayers and supplication in the Spirit. (Eph 6).

5. Providing Apostolic Warfare Mentorship

2 Timothy 2:3-4
You therefore must endure hardship as a good soldier of Jesus Christ. 4 No one engaged in warfare entangles himself with the affairs of this life, that he may please him who enlisted him as a soldier.

➢ Apostles and apostolic leaders prepare and develop people for war.

➢ The people of God are enlisted by virtue of salvation. Exo 15:3, Josh 5:13:15, Psa 18:34-35, Luke 22:36, 2Tim 2:3-4, Rev 19:11,13-15

6. Apostolic Warfare Intelligence

1 Peter 2:
11 Dearly beloved, I beseech you as strangers and pilgrims, abstain from fleshly lusts, which war against the soul.

\* Apostolic warning for high value target: the soul. Eph 6:12, Gal 3:1-2, 1Pet 2:1

* The enemy's battle route revealed: fleshly lust. 1 Peter 2:11-12, Gal 5: 19-21, 1John 2:16

7. Paul's Orders to Subordinate Commanders (pastors)

Ephesians 6:10-13

10 Finally, my brethren, be strong in the Lord, and in the power of his might.
11 Put on the whole armour of God, that ye may be able to stand against the wiles of the devil.
12 For we wrestle not against flesh and blood, but against principalities, against powers, against the rulers of the darkness of this world, against spiritual wickedness in high places.
13 Wherefore take unto you the whole armour of God that ye may be able to withstand in the evil day, and having done all, to stand.

- Apostle Paul gives out finally warfare orders (verse 10).

- Paul gives his leaders words of encouragement (verse 10).

- Paul gives an apostolic intelligence briefing (verse 12).

- Paul gives the proper battle dress for the ensuing battles (verse 11).

- He issues the battle position; to stand (verse 13).

Apostle and Apostolic Check-Up

1. **Apostles and apostolic individuals must be able to discern the battlefield. What do you see?**

   _____
   _____
   _____
   _____
   _____
   _____

2. Discernment and having a visionary perspective are paramount.
   What is the apostolic specialty you bring to your call or community as an apostle or apostolic ministry?

   _____
   _____

   1. If your vision or operations are church-focused, you are likely operating in the pastoral role rather than the apostolic. However, you can still operate apostolically!

   2. Understand that some apostles do not have churches under their leadership. Make your apostolic call and specialty more prominent than the number of churches under your authority.

   3. Your goal is not to get churches to submit to your authority; rather, your goal is to establish a relationship with the pastor or leader of the organization and influence it with apostolic paradigms.

4. The apostle should have the ability to help the Body of Christ perceive the three-dimensional aspects of God's will: the church's purpose and the Kingdom's destiny.

5. As an apostolic leader, ensure that you understand the ministry of fathering and the concept of spiritual family.

Apostolic Strategy Worksheet EXMAPLE

Date: _____

Work, Ministry, or Church Name: _____

Vision: _____
_____

Prophetic Word for this Strategy: _____
_____
_____
_____

Location of Strategy: _____

Describe Work:
_____
_____
_____
_____

Prophetic Confirmation # 1: _____
_____
_____
_____

Prophetic Confirmation # 2: _____
_____
_____
_____

Demographics for the Strategy's Area:   Attached  _____Yes  _____ No

Apostle/Covering advising you on Strategy: _____

Prophet advising you on Strategy: _____

Work's Estimate Start Date _____ Determine Start Date: _____

1st Year's Plan_____

_____

_____

_____

Apostolic Strategy Worksheet

Three Year's Plan

_____

_____

_____

_____

Work's Calling:          To Whom

                       _____

                       To What_____

                       To Where_____

Work's Genre: Affiliation _____ non-denomination _____
           Inter-denomination _____ Other _____

Parent Organizations: _____
_____

Work/Strategy's Mission Statement: _____

_____

_____

Strategy' Spiritual Issues and Concerns:

_____

_____
_____
_____
_____

Prayer Team Members:

_____
_____
_____
_____

Apostolic Strategy Worksheet

Prayer Team Members:

_____
_____
_____
_____

Training Goals:

_____
_____
_____

Business Goals:

_____
_____

Financial Team Members: _____
_____
_____
_____
_____

Financial Goals: _____
_____
_____
_____
_____

Course Name: Apostolic Church Structural Paradigm
Course Number: FAT-1200
Course Objective: To present a systematic approach for assisting a traditional church in transitioning into an apostolic body.

Scope:

Over the centuries, the Body of Christ has become bound to traditional systems. The issue with these systems is that they are often filled with man-made programs and denominational persuasions. Traditional church paradigms tend to be inward-focused serving only those inside while limiting access and relevance to those outside. They often restrict the freedom of the Holy Spirit and hinder the fulfillment of the Great Commission. Most importantly, they do not provide the best framework for nurturing the full growth and maturity of the believer or advancing the Kingdom of God.

Traditional Church Paradigm:

1. The structure, potential, and vitality of traditional church leadership are often built around a single individual.

2. If the hierarchical leader does not accept a particular gift, doctrine, or principle, their personal beliefs will dominate the vision and limit the growth of the local Body.

3. Apostolic fathering is typically absent in the traditional church model.

4. Many local gifts and talents remain unused and unrealized.
5. A controlling spirit is often present.

6. Leadership is trained primarily for the local assembly, not for global impact or the fulfillment of the Great Commission.

7. Traditionalism often fails to reflect true biblical Kingdom values.

8. Traditional models frequently mirror the Old Testament temple system the very structure and governance that resisted Jesus and His earthly ministry

Jesus
Apostle and High Priest of our profession

Apostle
Focus: Great commission, national and international ministry, hears from God for the direction of church.

Function: Est churches, develops sons of faith, selects and ordain senior pastors, establishes churches in assigned territory.

WORK TYPES:

| 1st Baptist | Austin Community Church | Greater Good Worship Center | 2nd Baptist | Community: |
|---|---|---|---|---|
| Territorial Generals | Regional Apostles | Apostolic Works | Specialty Apostolic | Specialty |

Snapshot of one of the apostle's works!

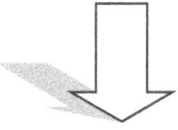

Senior Pastor (local church)
Focus: Receives guidance from apostle, local vision for region and communities.

Function: Develop and train regional and community pastors, assist the apostle in advancing the Great Commission vision, and select qualified regional and community pastors and leaders.

(1) Communities:

| Woods Subdivision | Pinewood Subdivision | Albany | Round Rock | Rose Wood Subdivision |

Note: Small group/regional pastors assigned by senior pastor; responsible for members in their assigned communities.

Functions of the Apostolic Church: From Pastorate to Laity Responsibilities

1. Corporate (weekly) worship
   Regular gatherings for unified worship and spiritual strengthening.

2. Church administration and operations
   Oversight of the organizational and business aspects of the church.

3. Holy convocations
   Special gatherings for consecration, alignment, and spiritual renewal.

4. Impartation of the five-fold ministry to the Body
   Equipping believers through the apostolic, prophetic, evangelistic, pastoral, and teaching offices.

5. Ordinations and activations
   Commissioning and empowering individuals for ministry and spiritual assignments.

6. Development of prophetic teams
   Training and deploying prophetic teams to serve regions, communities, and city-based small groups.

7. Spiritual fathering of the Body
   Providing covering, mentorship, and guidance for growth and maturity.

Benefits of the Apostolic Church:

1. Greater activation of spiritual gifts
   Spiritual gifts are stirred, recognized, and regularly exercised.

2. Development of individuals and ministry teams
   People are equipped and empowered to serve in their areas of calling.

3. Wider participation in ministry

   More members of the Body are able to function in their God-given roles.

4. Expanded territorial impact

   Apostolic ministry extends influence across communities, regions, and beyond.

5. Decentralized leadership

   Leadership is no longer limited to a rigid hierarchy, creating space for shared authority and function.

## Apostles and Apostolic Functions

| Regional Apostles | Specialty Apostles | Apostolic Works |
|---|---|---|
| 1. Have churches in specific define locations. | 1. Deliverance | 1. Community Ministries |
| 2. Have apostolic authority in that region. | 2. Faith | 2. Teaching Ministry. |
|  | 3. Teaching | 3. Evangelistic Ministry |
|  | 4. Spiritual Warfare |  |
|  | 5. Church Structure (foundation) |  |
|  | 6. Apostle Generals |  |
|  | 7. Apostle-Prophets |  |

Notes:

➢ Apostles are not lord over the pastors (apostles are servants in heart).

➢ Apostles submit to the authority of that house they are serving; apostles never usurp the set-man's house.

➢ Apostles earn the relationship of the houses they establish or the ones that comes under their authority.

➢ The apostle, apostle the pastor in private; never in front of his/her congregation.

Apostolic Connection to the Body

- Apostles are assigned by God to specific locations, regions, and nations. Pastors in those areas willingly submit to the apostle's leadership as led by the Spirit.

- Pastors and leaders oversee their own flocks and should not relinquish their authority to anyone. They receive apostolic insight and guidance from the apostle but retain pastoral responsibility.

Course Name             The Heart of the Apostolic Message
Course Number:          FAT-1300
Course Object:          Ensure, teach, and emphasis Jesus as the central apostolic message.
Scope:

In today's church, thousands of messages are preached from pulpits, many of them helpful and edifying. However, the core message must remain centered on Jesus and His Kingdom. Within the Body of Christ, there is a noticeable shortage of Christ-centered preaching. The apostolic message, by nature, places Jesus at the center. As an apostle or apostolic person, Jesus must be your central message not a side note, but the foundation of all you teach and impart.

1. Jesus is the Apostolic:

    1a. "Consider" Jesus is the Chief Apostle

    Hebrews 3: 1 Therefore, holy brethren, partakers of the heavenly calling, consider the Apostle and High Priest of our confession, Christ Jesus, consider: 1) to perceive, remark, observe, understand, 2) to consider attentively, fix one's eyes or mind upon.

    ➢ These scriptures highlight the essence of Jesus' apostleship; however, we often miss the depth and significance of it.

    ➢ Because we misunderstand His apostleship, we also have a limited understanding of the role of the apostle and by extension, the role of the five-fold ministry.

    ➢ As partakers in Christ, all believers are included in His apostolic mission.

1b.        Jesus the Apostolic Cornerstone.

Ephesians 2:

19 Now, therefore, you are no longer strangers and foreigners, but fellow citizens with the saints and members of the household of God,
20 having been built on the foundation of the apostles and prophets, Jesus Christ Himself being the chief cornerstone.

- The foundational doctrine of the apostles and prophets is the Gospel of Jesus Christ, the Son of God, and His Kingdom (see Matthew 2:4–14; Matthew 4:23; Luke 17:20–21; Ephesians 2:18–20).

- All doctrine within the Body of Christ should be shaped around the ministry, message, and life of Christ (see Romans 16:17–18; 1 Corinthians 3:11, 21; Galatians 1:6–8; 1 John 4:3).

- Vision statements, mission statements, and ministry goals must reflect Jesus as the central focus.

- The gospel of Jesus forms the foundation of the apostolic (law and Word), prophetic (prophecy concerning Jesus), and Kingdom message (see Psalm 46:4–5; Matthew 4:23; Luke 16:16).
- The Ascension Gifts Continually Speaks of the Apostolic Mandate

Ephesians 4:

9 (Now this, "He ascended"--what does it mean but that He also first descended into the lower parts of the earth? 10 He who descended is also the One who ascended far above all the heavens, that He might fill all things.) 11 And He Himself gave some to be apostles, some prophets, some evangelists, and some pastors and teachers, 12 for the equipping of the saints for the work of ministry, for the edifying of the body of Christ, 13 till we all come to the unity of the faith and of

the knowledge of the Son of God, to a perfect man, to the measure of the stature of the fullness of Christ;

- ➢ The ascension gifts represent the ongoing apostolic works of Jesus within the Church, continuing His mission during His physical absence (see Ephesians 4:11–12).

- ➢ All of the gifts require you to be sent to a specific place, for a specific purpose, and in a particular position for Christ.

- ➢ The Holy Spirit is the physical presence of the Godhead, enabling and empowering the apostolic gifts (see Job 16:19; Isaiah 42:1; Luke 4:18; Mark 13:11; John 3:5–6, 20:22; 1 John 4:4).

2a. Apostolic Mission of the Five-Fold Ministry

| Apostle: | Go establish where they are sent. |
|---|---|
| Prophet: | Go tell what they hear and see. |
| Evangelist: | Go tell the people the message of salvation. |
| Pastor: Go take care of the people. | |
| Teacher: | Go teach the people. |

1. The Apostle or Apostolic Ministry always emphasizes:

    1a. The Name of Jesus

    Acts 5: 28-32

    28 saying, "Did we not strictly command you not to teach in this name? And look, you have filled Jerusalem with your doctrine and intend to bring this Man's blood on us!" 29 But Peter and the other apostles answered and said: "We ought to obey God rather than men. 30 The God of our fathers raised up Jesus whom you murdered by hanging on a tree. 31 Him God has exalted to His right hand to be Prince and Savior, to give repentance to Israel and forgiveness of sins. 32 And we

are His witnesses to these things, and so also is the Holy Spirit whom God has given to those who obey Him."

- ✓ Always promotes the name and cause of Jesus.

- ✓ The focus of apostles and the apostolic message is Jesus.

- ✓ "He is risen" is the central apostolic message.

- ✓ God's purpose for His Kingdom is the second key subject.

1b. Teaches in the Name of Jesus

Acts 5:42, And daily in the temple, and in every house, they did not cease teaching and preaching Jesus as the Christ.

- ✓ Apostolic Teachers, daily, constantly teach apostolic doctrine.

- ✓ Apostolic believers teach in the home and temple (everywhere).

- ✓ Apostolic promotes and teaches in the name of Jesus.

- ✓ Apostolic teaches emphasizes Jesus and the kingdom message.

1c. He is the Son of God.

Acts 9: 20 Immediately he preached the Christ in the synagogues, that He is the Son of God.

1d. To abide in Christ's Doctrine.

2 John 1:

9 Whoever transgresses and does not abide in the doctrine of Christ does not have God. He who abides in the doctrine of Christ has both the Father and the Son.

- "Abide" refers to relationships or communion.

- Apostolic communion establishes a relationship with God, aligns you with His purpose, and connects you to His people.

1e.   The Apostolic Foundation of Jesus' Purpose

Luke 24:
46 Then He said to them, "Thus it is written, and thus it was necessary for the Christ to suffer and to rise from the dead the third day, 47 and that repentance and remission of sins should be preached in His name to all nations, beginning at Jerusalem. 48 And you are witnesses of these things. 49 Behold, I send the Promise of My Father upon you; but tarry in the city of Jerusalem until you are endued with power from on high."

One of Jesus' underlying purposes was to activate the Body into its apostolic mode of operation.

1f.   The Prototypical Apostolic Sermon

Ephesians 3: 8-19
To me, who am less than the least of all the saints, this grace was given, that I should preach among the Gentiles the unsearchable riches of Christ, 9 and to make all see what is the fellowship of the mystery, which from the beginning of the ages has been hidden in God who created all things through Jesus Christ; 10 to the intent that now the manifold wisdom of God might be made known by the church to the principalities and powers in the heavenly places, 11 according to the eternal purpose which He accomplished in Christ Jesus our Lord.

Prototypical Message Points:

- Directed to the Gentiles extending the message beyond Israel.
- Proclaiming the unsearchable riches of Christ centered on revealing Christ.

- Intended to make all see the mystery unveiling the hidden purpose of God.
- Reveals principalities and powers exposing spiritual forces and offering apostolic strategy for victory.

1h.  Major Apostolic Doctrinal Subjects:

Apostolic Doctrine Tenants

| Repentance | Baptism in Water | Resurrection |
|---|---|---|
| Sanctification | Justification by Faith | Faith |
| Baptism of Holy Spirit | Doctrine of Christ | Grace |
| Jesus': Birth, Life, | Death, Burial, | Resurrection, Ascension |
| Eternal Life | Kingdom Principles & Its Principles | Book of Revelations The Revelations of Jesus Christ |
| Eschatology: Doctrine of End Times | Discipleship | |

Course Name: Producing Apostolic Fruit
Course Number: FAT-1400
Course Objective: Developing next generation leaders.

Scope:

The ultimate objective of an apostle or apostolic leader is to:

1. Raise up the next generation of leaders and gifts within the Body.
2. Clearly understand their primary apostolic responsibility in fulfilling the assignment.
3. Produce apostolic fruit that shifts leaders' focus from self to equipping and edifying the Body.
4. Develop, implement, and direct an effective system that equips, trains, and activates people and their gifts.

1. For the apostle, there is no greater responsibility than raising sons in the faith. As apostolic leaders, we must refocus on this foundational aspect of our calling.

    1a. Among all the responsibilities of the apostle and apostolic leader, only one truly produces apostolic fruit: raising spiritual sons in the faith.

    1b. Apostles produce apostolic **sons** those who carry the DNA, vision, and function of the apostolic calling.

    1c. All apostolic leaders are called to reproduce after their own kind:
    - Apostles produce apostles,
    - Pastors produce pastors,
    - Teachers produce teachers,
    - Prophets produce prophets, and so on.

1. The First Consideration:

    Hebrews 3:

    1 Wherefore, holy brethren, partakers of the heavenly calling, **consider** the Apostle and High Priest of our profession, Christ Jesus.

> An apostolic leader must embrace humility, a heart of service, and unwavering commitment to the Father's purpose. (see Matthew 20:26; 1 Corinthians 3:18; 1 Corinthians 15:10; 2 Corinthians 3:5).

2a. Consider Jesus (Apostle)

Considers means: to perceive, remark, observe, understand to consider attentively, fix one's eyes or mind upon

We need to consider the apostolic nature of Jesus and His example of apostleship:

- Even though He was God the Son, as John the Baptist declared, "He is mightier than I," Jesus humbled Himself in every aspect.

- As the Son of God, He did not use His divine rights and privileges to override apostolic order but submitted fully to the Father's will.

2b. Considerations: You must carry the seed (fruit) before you can birth the fruit.

1. Jesus submitted to John the Baptist, whose ministry preceded His own.

   ❖ "Then Jesus came from Galilee to John at the Jordan to be baptized by him." (Matthew 3:13)

   ❖ Apostles and apostolic leaders must always walk in humility first.

2. Apostolic leaders and people are called to obey and submit to their current environments, laws, principles, and practices.

   ❖ In this example, Jesus honored existing protocol He did not bypass or break the law.

**1.** Jesus' ministry proceeded as John's ministry decreased.

> Matthew 4:
> 12 Now when Jesus heard that John had been put in prison, He departed to Galilee. 13 And leaving Nazareth, He came and dwelt in Capernaum, which is by the sea, in the regions of Zebulun and Naphtali, 14 that it might be fulfilled which was spoken by Isaiah the prophet, saying: 15 "The land of Zebulun and the land of Naphtali, By the way of the sea, beyond the Jordan, Galilee of the Gentiles: 16 The people who sat in darkness have seen a great light, And upon those who sat in the region and shadow of death Light has dawned." 17 From that time Jesus began to preach and to say, "Repent, for the kingdom of heaven is at hand."

The apostolic mission is not new; it is an extension of:

1. What the Holy Spirit is saying and doing in the present.
2. The current needs of the apostolic assignment.
3. The needs and vision mandates of the pastor.

3. First God Desires:

> Malachi 2:15 (New International Version)
> Has not [the LORD] made them one? In flesh and spirit, they are his. And why one? Because he was seeking godly offspring. So, guard yourself in your spirit, and do not break faith with the wife of your youth.

- ➢ The ultimately desire of God the Father is to have sons.

- ➢ As apostolic leaders we must have the same desire for offspring (sons).

3a. Sons Inherits

- Sons are the inheritors and the receptors of the Kingdom's blessings.

Romans 8:
14 For as many as are led by the Spirit of God, these are sons of God.

James 2:5
Listen, my dear brothers: Has not God chosen those who are poor in the eyes of the world to be rich in faith and to inherit the kingdom he promised those who love him?

Galatians 4:
7 Therefore you are no longer a slave but a son, and if a son, then an heir of God through Christ

3b. Sons Carry (Are Sent With) the Father's Business

- Sons carry forward the business of the family.
- Sons extend the father's legacy and posterity.
- Sons advance the father's life, mission, and purpose.
- Sons reflect the father's will, nature, and character.
- Sons are sent by the father, representing his authority and heart.

.4. The Father (precedence)
Spiritual fathers pass down the anointing of God to their spiritual son.

4a.     A Son's Request

2 Kings 2:

9 And so it was, when they had crossed over, that Elijah said to Elisha, "Ask! What may I do for you, before I am taken away from you?" Elisha said, "Please let a double portion of your spirit be upon me."

- ➤ Double portion is the sons portion.

- ➤ The request speaks of the relationship of Elijah and Elisha (spiritual father to spiritual son).

The Church can best be described as:

1. A family unit.
2. An extension of our Heavenly Father and His Son.
3. A conduit for God's holy purpose through the family of believers.
4. The visible expression of the Kingdom of God at hand.

4b.     A Father's Reply

2 Kings 2:

10 So he said, You have asked a hard thing. Nevertheless, if you see me when I am taken from you, it shall be so for you; but if not, it shall not be so." 11 Then it happened, as they continued on and talked, that suddenly a chariot of fire appeared with horses of fire, and separated the two of them; and Elijah went up by a whirlwind into heaven. 12 And Elisha saw it, and he cried out, "My father, my father, the chariot of Israel and its horsemen!" So, he saw him no more. And he took hold of his own clothes and tore them into two pieces.

- ✢ "See me" speaks of face-to-face intimacy and close spiritual connection.

- ✢ It should take God Himself to separate a spiritual father and son as seen when a chariot of fire and horses of fire separated Elijah and Elisha.

- A true son waits for the father's instruction before initiating their own works (see Luke 15:11–32).

4c. Spiritual Fathers are Foremost, Fruit Producer

2 Kings 2:
13 He also took up the mantle of Elijah that had fallen from him and went back and stood by the bank of the Jordan. 14 Then he took the mantle of Elijah that had fallen from him, and struck the water, and said, "Where is the Lord God of Elijah?" And when he also had struck the water, it was divided this way and that; and Elisha crossed over.

- ✓ What belongs to the Father is used to minister on His behalf not for personal purposes (John 12:49–50).

- ✓ Elisha ministered in the same way he observed from his spiritual father, Elijah (1 Corinthians 4:16; 11:1).

5. Jesus as Apostle

    5a. We must look at the Chief Apostle of our faith: Jesus. Great consideration must be observed in His Father to Son relationship. Observe in scriptures how the relationship drove Him from the cradle to the grave.

    John 12:
    49 For I have not spoken on My own authority; but the Father who sent Me gave Me a command, what I should say and what I should speak. 50 And I know that His command is everlasting life. Therefore, whatever I speak, just as the Father has told Me, so I speak."

- ✓ Jesus as God, did not and was not moved by His Deity, He exemplify His relationship with His Father, throughout His entire earthly ministry.

- ✓ As God the Creator, His very words and actions were apostolic.

5b. <u>Apostles and Sonship</u>

- ✦ Apostles are the spiritual fathers of the New Testament.

- ✦ They are responsible for passing down their God-given mantle to the next generation.

- ✦ Sonship is passed down through the processes of anointing, spiritual birthing, ordination, activation, and impartation.

5c. Apostle Paul as the Prototypical Apostolic father

1 Corinthians 4:
17 For this reason I have sent Timothy to you, who is my beloved and faithful son in the Lord, who will remind you of my ways in Christ, as I teach everywhere in every church.

- ✓ Apostolic sons are sons of faith (Galatians 3:6-9, 3:26).

- ✓ To qualify as a son, faithfulness must be a strong character trait (1 Corinthians 4:2; Revelation 2:10).

- ✓ Faithfulness will be the hallmark and cornerstone of a true apostolic child (Psalm 26:2; James 1:3, 12).

- ✓

Philippians 2:

**19** But I trust in the Lord Jesus to send Timothy to you shortly, that I also may be encouraged when I know your state. **20** For I have no one **like-minded**, who will sincerely care for your state. **21** For all seek their own, not the things which are of Christ Jesus. **22** But you know **his proven character**, that as a son with his father **he served** with me in the gospel.

- ➢ Like-minded sons seek the things of their father.

- ➢ Sons have proven character.

- ➢ Sons serve.

**1Timothy 1:**

**2** To Timothy, **a true son** in the faith: Grace, mercy, and peace from God our Father and Jesus Christ our Lord. **3** As I urged you when I went into Macedonia-- remain in Ephesus that you may charge some that they **teach no other doctrine.**

- ➢ Apostolic sons are true sons.

- ➢ True apostolic sons will teach their fathers doctrine only.

Course Name:        Apostolic Kingdom
Course Number:      FAT-1500
Course Objective:   To bridge the kingdom with its apostolic purpose.

Note: For a more extensive coverage of the Kingdom, please refer to the Apostolic-Kingdom Workbook.

Scope:

> The subject of the Kingdom is broad and profound, far too vast to be fully explored within this single lesson. My aim here is to offer a bridge between the apostolic and the Kingdom, helping to illuminate the close, hand-in-hand relationship between the two.

A foundational study for anyone engaged in the Apostolic Kingdom is the study of Jesus' Kingdom principles.

- ❖ You cannot effectively carry out your apostleship or apostolic ministry without a solid understanding of the Kingdom of God and its principles (John 3:10, 16–17).

- ❖ It is possible to function, to some degree, as a traditional church or apostolic ministry without a clear understanding of the Kingdom of Heaven.

- ❖ However, if this is the case, you risk robbing both the people and you of your local church's full destiny and spiritual heritage.

1. We must first define the two different realms of the kingdom.

   The Kingdom of God encompasses all territories and realms both created and uncreated, visible and invisible. It is far vast than the Kingdom of Heaven, the universe, or the earth.

Kingdom of God: Reality:

1. All beings are subjected
2. Creation                              (Creator)
3. Gives Life                            (Zoe of God)
4. Resurrects                         (The Resurrector)
5. Ownership                       (Sovereign)
6. Creates                               (His will, His Word)
7. Holds the waters of the world in the palms of His hands.    Lord/Master
8. Calls things that be not          The Word (Yeshua)
9. Framed the worlds by His words.   The Word (Yeshua)
10. Owns cattle on a thousand hills.   Master

**2.** The Kingdom of Heaven: (it's fluid).

2a.    It's the rule, realm, and the influence of God in the matters of man.

2b.    The Kingdom of Heaven is within the Kingdom of God.

Benefits of the Kingdom of Heaven (being at hand)

1. Empowers                 Acts 1:8, Luke 10:19-20
2. Five-Fold Ascension Gifts    Eph 4:11
3. Gives Body its Authority      Matt 11:24, Luke 10:19, Rev 12:11
4. Gives Offices               Eph 4:8,11
5. The Apostolic              Matthew 28:19, mark 3:13-19,
6. The Church                 Acts 2: 1-4
7. Fruits of the Holy Spirit       Gal 5:22-23
8. Gifts of Holy Spirit           1Cor 12:1-10
9. Ambassadorship            2Cor 5:20
10. Discipleship                **1Pet 3:15, Luke 14:25-35**
11. Sonship                      **Gal 4:1-7**

3. **FUNDAMENTALLY THE KINGDOM.**

    Luke 4:

    43 but He said to them, "I must preach the kingdom of God to the other cities also, because for this purpose I have been sent."

    - ✓ Jesus was sent *apostolically* for a Kingdom purpose (Daniel 7:14; Matthew 18:11; John 6:38).

    - ✓ Jesus' messages consistently centered on the Kingdom His preaching, teaching, and parables all illustrated the Kingdom's mandate (Matthew 5–7).

    - ✓ The apostolic nature and works operate on behalf of the Kingdom (John 3:8).

    - ✓ Kingdom people are ambassadors of the Apostolic Kingdom (2 Corinthians 5:20; Luke 10:1).

    - ✓ Jesus' apostolic (sent) death and resurrection serve as the bridge between people and the Kingdom (Hebrews 4:16).

4. **THE ORIGINAL APOSTLES WERE ACTIVATED INTO HIS SAME PURPOSE BY HIMSELF.**

    Luke 9:

    1 Then He called His twelve disciples together and gave them power and authority over all demons, and to cure diseases. 2 He sent them to preach the kingdom of God and to heal the sick. 3 And He said to them, "Take nothing for the journey, neither staff nor bag nor bread nor money; and do not have two tunics apiece

    - ✓ They were chosen as disciples, developed into apostles, trained in the purpose of the Kingdom, and sent out on its behalf.

**5. WHERE DO TODAY'S APOSTLES GET THEIR AUTHORITY?**

Matthew 21:

23 Now when He came into the temple, the chief priests and the elders of the people confronted Him as He was teaching, and said, "By what authority are You doing these things? And who gave You this authority?" 24 But Jesus answered and said to them, "I also will ask you one thing, which if you tell Me, I likewise will tell you by what authority I do these things: 25 The baptism of John--where was it from? From heaven or from men?" And they reasoned among themselves, saying, "If we say, 'From heaven,' He will say to us, 'Why then did you not believe him?' 26 But if we say, 'From men,' we fear the multitude, for all count John as a prophet." 27 So they answered Jesus and said, "We do not know." And He said to them, "Neither will I tell you by what authority I do these things.

28 "But what do you think? A man had two sons, and he came to the first and said, 'Son, go, work today in my vineyard.' 29 He answered and said, 'I will not,' but afterward he regretted it and went. 30 Then he came to the second and said likewise. And he answered and said, 'I go, sir,' but he did not go. 31 Which of the two did the will of his father?" They said to Him, "The first." Jesus said to them, "Assuredly, I say to you that tax collectors and harlots enter the kingdom of God before you.

- We receive our Kingdom purpose through the messages of Jesus (Matthew 28:18–20).

- We are reborn into our Kingdom purpose (Revelation 1:5–6).

- Our role as Kingdom ambassadors is the source of our authority within the Church (John 3:1–9).

- The Great Commission empowers us both apostolically and legally to carry out Kingdom work—whether in foreign territories, spiritual warfare, governmental matters, or global missions.

Course Name: Why we Fail (not the church)
Course Number: FAT-1600
Course Objective: To discuss the church failure.

Scope:

Success for the Church is not measured by buildings, mega-ministries, or financial gain. To be clear, I am not labeling the Church a failure, nor dismissing the completed and ongoing work of Christ. Rather, our failure is not individual but collective rooted in our tendency to miss God's will and purpose for the Church's formation and commission.

There is an entire world the Church is failing to reach. Why?

We, as leaders, are often failing to effectively reach and equip our own members. Why?

Many members remain spiritually undernourished and lack proper development as disciples or leaders. Why?

1. **HIERARCHY POSITIONS**

    Due to television and various forms of media, the roles of Pastor and Evangelist have been highly venerated in the public eye. As a result, these positions are often glamorized, leading many to desire them for the wrong reasons.

    In contrast, the apostolic emphasizes serving rather than lording. Its focus is on fulfilling the Great Commission not on personal prestige, power, or position.

1a. Church Structure by Paradigms:

| Traditional Hierarchy Positions | The Apostolic Church |
|---|---|
| a. Bishop | a. Apostle |
| b. Senior Pastorate | b. Prophet |
| c. Pastor | c. Teacher |
| d. Superintendent | |
| e. Elders | |
| f. Preachers | |
| g. Ministers | |

2. LEADERS ARE NOT FOCUS ON THE DEVELOPMENT OF THEIR MEMBERS.

2a. Many leaders fail to develop other leaders and prepare the next generation (2 Corinthians 13:12–16).

2b. Because the church or ministry is structured within a hierarchical system, the leader often operates based on personal feelings and opinions about individuals and situations.

2c. The office of the apostle and the apostolic calling require intentional development.

- Fathering, discipling, and mentoring the membership are essential responsibilities for any leader.

CHURCH IS BUILT ON A DEPENDENT SYSTEM (THE PASTOR IS MAIN PLAYER).

As mentioned earlier, the Church is traditionally built around the pastoral position. In this system, everything tends to filter through this one individual.

This structure often produces, at best, sons and daughters of the faith who are weak, lack confidence, and are unprepared to assume apostolic authority. In turn, they fail to produce spiritual fruit. At worst, they become introverted replacements, following in the footsteps of their predecessors.

Dependent Issues:

1. Every major decision must pass through the traditional pastor or the organization's leader.

2. There is often no properly trained successor to carry the vision forward.

3. The vision of the Church becomes limited to the perspective of this one leader.

4. The local body's spiritual growth can be constrained by the limitations of this leader.

4. The Church Doesn't Reflect the Humility of God.

1. Today's Church often misses the apostolic essence. A core element of the apostolic calling is humble service, yet the traditional Church does not fully reflect this humility.

2. The apostolic mandate that represents Jesus is always centered on Him and His purpose. The apostolic is about serving others, not seeking personal gain or glory.

3. **CHURCH IS DIVIDED.**

This is one of the saddest realities of the Church: we appear divided to the world. We have white churches, black churches, Asian churches, churches with differing doctrines and opinions, and so on.

✓ The apostolic order, however, exemplifies unity.

4. LEADERS DON'T UNDERSTAND THE APOSTOLIC ROLE OF THE BODY.

This issue is at the root of many of the Body's problems. We have numerous leaders heading churches and ministries who lack understanding of the apostolic role or the role of apostles in the Body. Many of these leaders are uneducated, lack spiritual insight, are overly focused on denominationalism, and are bound by tradition.

This issue is essentially a dysfunction within the apostolic family. Without spiritual fathers, the family of God has developed a worldly character, leading to a pseudo-church model that hinders growth and effectiveness.

Course Name:    Requirements to be an Apostolic Body
Course Number:  FAT-1700
Course Objective:   Open Discussion: Biblical Search
Scope:

There are essential spiritual prerequisites to becoming an apostle, an apostolic person, or an apostolic body. This vital area of ministry cannot be approached with only a partial understanding or application of biblical principles.

You Must:

- Receive a direct call from Jesus.
- Believe in and be baptized in the Holy Spirit, with the evidence of speaking in tongues.
- Receive apostolic revelation.
- Fully believe in the five-fold ministry offices (Ephesians 4:11).
- Believe in and practice all the fruits of the Spirit.
- Have a pastor or leader who has undergone a prophetic-apostolic shift in their ministry.
- Believe in and operate in all the gifts of the Holy Spirit.
- Accept and uphold all biblical principles.
- Embrace the Gospel of the Kingdom.
- Possess sound revelation and understanding of eschatology.

Course Name:     Your Specific Apostolic Sphere of Influence
Course Number:   FAT-1800
Course Objective: Understand apostles and apostolic boundaries and platforms.

Note:

"Realms of influence" or territory are often among the most misunderstood responsibilities of a leader. Even if God has called you to be an apostle, prophet, evangelist, pastor, teacher, minister, or leader, you must understand the specific realm of your influence.

A minister or leader must recognize that they are not the minister or leader of the entire Body. There is wisdom and safety in this understanding it encourages accountability and submission to those in authority when operating outside of your localized assignment.

Realms of Influence: Considerations Before Creeping

Before stepping into a new realm of influence, carefully consider the following:

a. Anointing Do you carry the anointing specifically needed to reach and impact that realm?

b. Spiritual Authority – Do you possess the spiritual "generalship" necessary to confront and overcome the demonic powers operating in that realm?

c. Relational Connectivity – Have you established meaningful relationship and connection with the leaders and people of that realm?

d. Foundational Authority – Have you been given the authority and grace to lay or build upon a foundation in that territory?

e. Doctrinal Authority – Are you equipped and authorized to rightly divide and clarify the Word of God in that context?

f.   Prophetic Direction – Have you received a prophetic word giving you specific "orders" or direction to engage?

g.   Spiritual Release – Has the Holy Spirit spoken release through your governing authority, spiritual covering, or leader to go?

PLATFORMS

ROMANS 15:20
Yea, so have I strived to preach the gospel, not where Christ was named lest I should build upon another man's foundation:

> Paul made it a point to go where no one else had preached, so that he would not be building on another person's foundation.

a.   Unless God grants you a specific platform to operate from, you cannot assume it on your own.

Example:   Evangelist Billy Graham was a global evangelist this platform was given to him by the grace of God.

b.   No one can establish a platform of their own authority. Unless God establishes your platform, you are limited to the realm of your local assignment.

## The Fruit and Results Of Faulty Platforms Or Foundations:

a.   Carnality
b.   Babes in Christ
c.   Only able to drink the milk of the Word, but not yet able to eat the meat of the Word.
d.   Envying
e.   Strife
f.   Division

2. Specific Platforms (Example Apostle Paul's)

Examples:

Romans 11:13
For I speak to you Gentiles, inasmuch as <u>I am the apostle of the Gentiles</u>, I magnify mine office:

1 Corinthians 9: 1-2
Am I not an apostle? am I not free? have I not seen Jesus Christ our Lord? are not <u>ye my work in the Lord</u>? 2 If I be not an apostle unto others, yet doubtless I am to you: for the seal of mine apostleship are ye in the Lord.

- ✓ Paul's platform is the Gentiles.

- ✓ Paul's platform is his office.

3. The Twelve Platform

   a. The Twelve were specifically groomed by Jesus for the Church. They were prepared as foundational apostles to help launch the Church and propel it beyond its comfort zones and boundaries. An in-depth study of their journeys reveals that each of the Twelve had a distinct assignment, a unique platform from which to operate.

3. Platform Shifts

   A leader must understand when and where an apostolic platform shift is. If he or she is not discerning, they will walk in an area or realm in error and without proper authority. That is the reason why you hear the apostle Paul states, "If I be not an apostle unto others". He understood apostolic platform shifts. He understood that to some he was not their apostle. More than anything he understood that as he was "sent" there was and is times and places he was not called to apostle that place or people.

a.	First, the Apostle Peter was the leader of the church in Jerusalem.

Acts15:7
And when there had been much disputing, Peter rose up, and said unto them, Men and brethren, ye know how that a good while ago God made choice among us, that the Gentiles by my mouth should hear the word of the gospel and believe.

b.	Later you observe a shift in the leadership platform in the church in Jerusalem.

(From the Apostle Peter leadership to the Apostle James leadership)

Acts 21: 17-26
17 And when we were come to Jerusalem, the brethren received us gladly. 18 And the day following Paul went in with us unto James; and all the elders were present. 19 And when he had saluted them, he declared particularly what things God had wrought among the Gentiles by his ministry. 20 And when they heard it, they glorified the Lord, and said unto him, Thou seest, brother, how many thousands of Jews there are which believe ; and they are all zealous of the law: 21 And they are informed of thee, that thou teachest all the Jews which are among the Gentiles to forsake Moses, saying that they ought not to circumcise their children, neither to walk after the customs. 22 What is it therefore? the multitude must needs come together: for they will hear that thou art come.

23 Do therefore this that we say to thee: We have four men which have a vow on them; 24 Them take, and purify thyself with them, and be at charges with them, that they may shave their heads: and all may know that those things, whereof they were informed concerning thee, are nothing; but that thou thyself also walkest orderly, and keepest the law.

- ✓ In this passage of Scripture, the Apostle James instructs the Apostle Paul to purify himself according to the customs of the platform from which James operates.

- ✓ The Apostle Paul submits (rightly so) because he is not operating within his own apostolic platform to the Gentiles but is instead on the Jewish platform overseen by the Apostle James.

25 As touching the Gentiles which believe, we have written and concluded that they observe no such thing, save only that they keep themselves from things offered to idols, and from blood, and from strangled, and from fornication. 26 Then Paul took the men, and the next day purifying himself with them entered into the temple, to signify the accomplishment of the days of purification, until that an offering should be offered for every one of them.

- ✝ Here we see that the Apostle James did not place the burden of Jewish laws on the Gentiles, as doing so would have been a violation of territorial or platform boundaries.

4. How God Deploys Apostles Today

- ✓ If you review Lesson FAT 1200, *The Apostolic Church Structure Paradigm*, you will find an example of an apostolic church structure that includes leaders from various denominational and cultural backgrounds.

✓ It's important to understand that an apostle is not meant to assimilate into the pastorate or take over the church or ministry to which they are assigned nor should that ministry assimilate the apostle. The biblical model is for the Body of Christ to function apostolically, aligned with God's Kingdom purpose. For this to happen, all parties must understand how God deploys apostles in the Church today.

In FAT 1200, we discussed the "authoritative" platforms that God divinely assigns, and how these platforms impact your ability to operate and influence at different levels.

    a. The Platform
    b. Specific Platforms
    c. The Twelve's Platforms
    d. Platform Shifts

4.a Apostles and Apostolic Usages

    4a1. Apostle-Fathers

    Apostolic fathers hold the premier role and responsibility in any and all apostleships. This specific type of apostle raises spiritual sons in the faith, develops pastors, and teaches and articulates foundational doctrine within their assigned sphere of responsibility.

    Apostolic fathers serve as the spiritual lineage essential for the proper propagation of the Body of Christ. The apostle plays a key role in raising the next generation of leaders, ensuring they are properly integrated into the Body. Most importantly, the absence of an Apostolic Father mirrors the absence of fathers in the natural family.

4a2. Territorial-Apostle

Territorial apostles are assigned to specific areas and regions, exercising significant spiritual power and authority over the principalities in that region.

These apostles serve in many areas within the Kingdom of God and demonstrate great signs and miracles in their ministry. They are considered specialists within the Kingdom, ordained, anointed, or endowed with supernatural abilities to operate on various levels.

Territorial Assignments:
a. Deliverance Ministry
b. Supernatural Faith Deposits in that region.
c. Healing
d. Open Territorial Platforms (government, business, church).

4a3. Strategic-Apostle

Strategic apostles are the "warring" (front-line) apostles. These apostles can discern both current and future battlefields. They play a crucial role in helping align and realign the vision and efforts of the Body in accordance with the Great Commission.

Strategic apostles assist local pastors with directional ministry and reveal the demonic strategies of principalities, helping to devise plans to overcome their attacks.

4a4. Apostle-Prophets

Apostle-Prophets are leaders who operate apostolically while also possessing a prophetic office and anointing. These individuals function with a "corporate" prophetic anointing, seeing and operating from a broader, Kingdom perspective.

They are instrumental in birthing and fathering other prophets with a Great Commission mindset. Apostle-Prophets establish the apostolic-prophetic presbytery within the Kingdom.

4a5. Apostle-Pastors

Apostle-Pastors are those who establish and raise other churches. While they may be pastors themselves, they are often not recognized as apostles. They possess the gift of planting, building, and organizing churches. Historically, apostolic pastors may have several church plants and though not formally called apostles, operate as apostle-pastors.

4a6. Apostles-Evangelist

Apostle-Evangelists are apostolic evangelists who birth, father, and raise up evangelists for the Kingdom and the Great Commission. They raise spiritual sons not for the church, but for the advancement of the Kingdom of God. These apostles operate from a God-given platform, entering into courts, kingdoms, governments, and nations to bring salvation to the people.

4a7. Apostle-Teacher

Apostle-Teachers are those who have a God-given platform to teach apostolic and Kingdom doctrine, with a focus on the Great Commission. This apostle also births and raises spiritual sons in the faith to be teachers. They are anointed specifically to teach apostolic doctrine. The platform they are given allows them to teach at various levels, depending on the opportunities and doors that platform provides.

www.ingramcontent.com/pod-product-compliance
Lightning Source LLC
LaVergne TN
LVHW061936070526
838199LV00060B/3850